Never Too Late To Be Loved

How One Couple Under Stress Discovered Intimacy and Joy

BY

Browne Barr

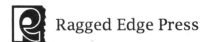 Ragged Edge Press

This Ragged Edge Press publication
was printed by
Beidel Printing House, Inc.
63 West Burd Street
Shippensburg, PA 17257 USA

In respect for the contents contained herein, the acid-free paper used in this book meets the guidelines for permanence and durability of the Committee on Production Guidelines for Book Longevity of the Council on Library Resources.

This book is sold with the understanding that neither the author nor the publisher is engaged in rendering legal or professional advice.

For a complete list of available publications
please write
Ragged Edge Press
Division of White Mane Publishing Company, Inc.
P.O. Box 152
Shippensburg, PA 17257 USA

Library of Congress Cataloging-in-Publication Data

Barr, Browne
        Never too late to be loved: how one couple, under stress,
    discovered intimacy and joy / by Browne Barr.
            p.   cm.
        ISBN 1-57249-035-7 (alk. paper)
        1. Remarriage--United States--Case studies.   2. Remarried people-
    -Religious life--United States--Case studies.   3. Stepfamilies-
    -United States--Case studies.   4. Terminally ill--United States-
    -Family relationships-- Case studies.   5. Barr, Elizabeth.
    I. Title.
    HQ536.B3237   1996
    646.7'8--dc20   96-19410
                                                              CIP

Without exception all the persons in this story truly exist or once did. I present them here as I experienced them. They would doubtless like a few footnotes or a face lift here and there. They have not been granted that privilege. I take responsibility for the good or ill you may see in them. I wish also to record my gratitude to Richard E. Levy, Ph.D., and Mary Ann Hedin without whose skill and patience this story would never have come into focus or into print.

Knights Valley   Browne Barr
Easter 1996

TABLE OF CONTENTS

PROLOGUE
Before the Beginning and After the Ending vii

CHAPTER 1
Let My People Go 1

CHAPTER 2
A Bow Is Set in the Cloud; A Promise Is Made 7

CHAPTER 3
Taken Away to Die in the Wilderness? 17

CHAPTER 4
"Is There No Balm in Gilead;
Is There No Physician There?" 23

CHAPTER 5
Some Have Compassion, Making a Difference 28

CHAPTER 6
If I Make My Bed in Hell..37

CHAPTER 7
Better Is a Handful of Quietness,
Than Two Hands Full of Toil..44

CHAPTER 8
Make to Yourselves Friends 51

CHAPTER 9
Would God It Were Morning 56

CHAPTER 10
My Soul Is Cast Down Within Me 63

CHAPTER 11
Bring Quickly the Best Robe 70

CHAPTER 12
My Harp Is Tuned for a Dirge 78

CHAPTER 13
Be Angry But Do Not Sin 82

CHAPTER 14
Do Not Let the Sun Go Down on Your Anger 87

CHAPTER 15
Exceeding Great and Precious Promises 92

CHAPTER 16
Friends Who Stick Closer than a Brother 102

CHAPTER 17
Better to Marry than to Burn 109

CHAPTER 18
Eating the Bread of Idleness 114

CHAPTER 19
As a Sparrow Alone upon the Housetop 121

CHAPTER 20
Creeping Things and Flying Fowl 128

CHAPTER 21
The Heights of the Mountains Are His Also 139

CHAPTER 22
Aaron and Hur Held Up His Hands
So They Were Steady Until Sunset 150

CHAPTER 23
But on the Seventh Day You Shall Rest 157

CHAPTER 24
Is Not the Body More than the Clothing? 166

CHAPTER 25
Therefore . . . Let Us Love One Another 177

POEM – "A LIST COMPOSED ON SACRED GROUND" 184

EPILOGUE
After the Ending and Before the Beginning 185

PROLOGUE

Before the Beginning
and After the Ending

When I returned from the cemetery I met Frank Mueller, our young physician, in the short hallway which connects the kitchen and our bedroom, the room with the great window looking out at Mt. St. Helena. We met there in the space which had separated Elizabeth and me momentarily when she returned from the visit to Frank's office six years earlier with his gentle but clear words about the deteriorating condition of her heart and lungs.

Frank and I stopped abruptly there in the passageway as we met. We looked at each other and then Frank said, "Guess it's time for us to talk."

"Talk?" I asked.

"Yes," he replied.

"About what?"

"About us. About what has happened to us."

"Sure," I said, not quite sensing what he had in mind.

So we stepped into the bedroom, away from the many guests visiting on the patio. I hugged him and thanked him and he hugged me, I guess. But mostly we just stood and looked at each other.

It was very awkward. Some words passed between us. I do not remember them. I remember not feeling as I thought a man should feel who has just come home from burying his wife. I was disappointed that all my thoughts were trivial. I felt like a person going on about the weather when the weather is nothing much to talk about, just ordinary weather.

Frank later told me that he felt that something good passed between us that day, standing in the bedroom with the immense window, in the bedroom where his life and ours had first intersected, in the bedroom where only a few days earlier, on the bed with the bone colored sheets embellished with immense butterflies, orange and blue and black and yellow, Elizabeth had died . . . alone.

I wondered what he thought had happened to us.

That happening was not there for me, whatever it was, or so I thought. But it was there all the time. There for me, but hidden from me. And it has never gone away. I have mused endlessly about it. It has grown since in beauty and power. Something incredibly wonderful had happened to Elizabeth and me. Actually there was no doubt in my mind about that even then. But it was not named. I couldn't identify it. And until something is named you cannot really possess it or deal with it.

Months have passed since that September day, but my wondering about that encounter in which Frank proposed we talk about what had happened to us, has not. It will not stop haunting me. It will not let me off, permit me to dismiss it, forget it. My failure to understand it has felt like a failure to understand why the last six years of a beleaguered marriage, rocked by illness and conflict and disappointment, turned out to be so beautiful with a special glory all their own.

I have kept thinking about Frank's question. I have kept searching for the answer. I have kept sensing that in that answer is a gift ready for me to claim, maybe a gift to share. But I cannot possess it until I can name it. And I cannot share it until I possess it.

In recent weeks some of the wrapping hiding that gift has begun to fall away. I am excited by the emerging outline, the warm color. The clues have been there all along, sticking up here and there through the story of the last six years of our marriage. They are time and space clues, ordinary things and ordinary people, in ordinary time and ordinary space. God, too. Ruminating on the story and following those clues I brushed up against the answer, something quite common but beautiful almost beyond any telling of it. But I shall try.

What had happened to us was very simple. We had experienced the aging of our love! That was it. But that is so prosaic, so worn, so weary sounding. Aging of love? Are there no fresher words? But "aging" it was, like wine slowly brought to its perfect moment. And "love" it was, too; but there are so many kinds of love. Which of three do we claim: erotic, philia, agape? Sensual, friendship, self-giving? Must we make a choice? Take one and send the others flying!

Is love somehow split up into three parts like all Gaul for the convenience of theological cartographers? Or do these distinctions really match our human experience? Are these three experiences the unfolding of love toward its consummate possibility, the everlasting arms, ultimate intimacy? Are these three experiences of love, each with passion and color and pain, offered for the nurturing of the inner person, each opening unto the next with movement back and forth as long as we live, for those trusting enough to venture? Erotic love, friendship love, self-giving love.

It was mostly this last kind of love that was at the heart of the happening in our final six years together. Although anyone could see the other kinds of love were there as well. But it was this "agape" love that was dealing with us. We did not invite it or welcome it and it was not all sweetness and light anymore than the experience of erotic love is or friendship love. But here it was, love that takes the initiative and enters into the pain of another. But we could have missed it. We almost did. Amazing Grace!

It came to us through each other but through many other people too, very ordinary people like us. And its presence was manifested in many ways but most remarkably by two human capacities within us and others for which it supplied fresh energy: the capacity to receive and to give forgiveness; and the capacity to receive and to make promises.

If I were as wise and learned as the late Hannah Arendt, I would not need a whole book to share this joyous and liberating happening with you. I would just remind us all, as she has, that whatever our age or circumstance *forgiveness releases us from the irreversibility of the past, and promises deliver us from the unpredictability of the future.* Then I would add a couple of profound sentences like hers in *The Human Condition* where she says, in effect,

> *Without being* forgiven
> *released from the consequences of what we have done*
> *we remain its victims forever.*
> *Without being bound to the fulfillment of* promises
> *we would be condemned*
> *to wander helplessly*
> *and without direction in the darkness*
> *of each man's lonely heart.*

Both faculties, therefore
Forgiving *and* Promising
depend on the presence and acting of others
for no one can forgive himself
and no one can be bound by a promise
made only to himself.

However, I am not as wise or learned as Ms. Arendt. I can only share this happening with you by telling you a story of forgiveness and promise from beginning to end. It's a different kind of love story, but it is a love story. It is a love story which is no respecter of age. It is a story of the aging of love, the deepening of love. In some chapters there is a hint, a private disclosure of the ultimate intimacy.

Our story begins on the day we moved to the California wine country to launch the glorious years of retirement. But to understand where we were on that day, we have to go back before that beginning. I need to risk putting on display some of the furniture and china, inner and outer, with which we arrived at the threshold of age. More than that, I suspect I may have to display some we should have been rid of long before that beginning. So maybe this story really doesn't have a beginning. Except "in the beginning God."

Be that as it may, let's begin anyway.

CHAPTER 1

Let My People Go

Elizabeth and I spent much of our honeymoon in the New Haven, Connecticut, city dump. We were there not because we had agreed upon what furniture and china we should discard. We were there not because we thought it would be a good place to sit and review the attitudes we needed to dump. We were there on an outing of sorts.

We began making visits to the New Haven dump in August of 1957 because Elizabeth ruptured a spinal disc earlier that summer, a few weeks after we were married. Her first outdoor adventures during convalescence from surgery were trips with me to the public dump. We both had been widowed. My wife had died of cancer when our children were four and six years old. Elizabeth's husband had drowned when she was four months pregnant with their second child. She had been struggling for ten years as a single mother, living with her parents. I had been struggling for five years as a single father, with the help of a housekeeper.

In the summer of 1956 when my son, Christopher, was ten and my daughter, Sue, was eight, I took them to Maine to visit the friends who had introduced me to their mother. I felt that Barbara Cushman, a consummate matchmaker, who had been my wife's roommate at the Eastman School of Music, and her husband, Bob, who had conspired with her, had some responsibility

1

to help me care for the children of that marriage while my house-keeper had her annual vacation. It didn't bother me a bit to move in on them and invade their privacy.

However, this summer they sounded unusually eager for me to come. I had not been there long before I discovered why. In the cottage next door was a charming petite school teacher from Georgia, who baked incredibly flaky fresh blueberry pies and who knew the Latin names of every growing thing on that forested hillside above the lobster laden waters of the Maine coast.

"You must meet her right away," Barbara urged. "She has beautiful big brown eyes."

"And two beautiful big hungry growing costly children," Bob filled in.

"No way," I protested. "You have trapped me."

"Nonsense," said Barbara, "wouldn't think of it. You know we have never interfered in your affairs. Or given you advice." She laughed and threw me a playful kiss. "But we have arranged a picnic for tonight."

"What's her name?" I asked with feigned resignation. "And when do we meet?"

Barbara then laid out the plan with the concise brevity and authority of the competent manager. "Bob's taking you fishing this afternoon in the boat he has leased for the summer. He's crazy for you to see it. When you've had your fill, come on over and meet us at the beach at the end of the bay. Come when you like but be there at five. Her name is Elizabeth and she and I will bring the food and the kids and meet you there. And we're not having lobster so don't get your hopes up."

"You've got it all set up, haven't you, my dear little manipulator."

"I certainly have," Barbara replied, "and if you want me to help you with Chris and Sue for two weeks, you sure had better cooperate."

So it was that Elizabeth and I met. Later she told me that when Bob and I came in toward shore in the boat, it took her a moment to realize that I was only standing up in the boat, not walking on the water. She had resisted Barbara's enthusiasm to that moment, expecting me to be some frail bookish type who spoke with a Gothic accent. She had never met a Yale Divinity School professor before. Well, it is true, that I have never been stopped on the street by a Hollywood scout, hunting a fresh mati-nee idol, but Elizabeth, remembering that meeting, claimed that I had thick black curly hair, was over six feet tall, and did not yet need to diet. As for me, when I saw her standing on the beach with binoculars in her hand, talking with Barbara, I thought, not bad, not bad at all for a Southern Baptist schoolteacher, but so small, why she won't even come to my armpit.

Bob ran the boat up onto the beach and I stepped out and forthwith fell almost flat out in the soft wet sand. When my children, encouraged by the older Cushman children, began to snicker, it became obvious I was not hurt and Barbara joined them in the nervous hilarity. But it was not at Barbara's feet I had fallen. I looked up straight into large dark eyes and at that moment Elizabeth smiled.

There was an ominous silence. I just knelt there in the wet sand until I realized I was staring at her. Her face was not in any way extraordinary but the smile changed everything, drawing little bright rays of light out of every corner of her eyes and crevice of her face. "You must be Browne Barr," she said, offering me her hand as I tried to stand up and collect myself. "You fell very gracefully."

"Thanks," I croakingly whispered, as I regained my feet and then my voice.

Strange, isn't it, how reliable the information is which your gut supplies! I knew in that instant of her speaking that this little, full-figured, southern-speaking young woman and I had a future, beginning now when we both were just on the edge of 40.

Her children were there, too. Her son, Layton, was nine. In age, poor boy, he was squeezed in between my two. The three of them were eleven months apart, a fact which provided them and us a lot of amusement at various times in the years which followed. Elizabeth's daughter, Leigh, was 13 and already giving full and fair warning of the troubles she and we would have with boys for the next few years.

At the beach encounter Layton and Leigh seemed to stand back in their mother's shadow. I felt they viewed me as a grievous threat. It turned out quite otherwise. They saw me as their liberator. They lived with their grandparents, which was all very well but it was not like other kids. In the years to come the two sets of children had many arguments about which was worse—to be reared by grandparents or a housekeeper, by a single mother or a single father, or, alas, in a bonded family.

As the picnic moved through its early awkward stages to the more relaxed time with everyone happily fed, I kept feeling a romance was inevitable if only all four children would behave. A few nights later, when Elizabeth and I started down the hill in my station wagon for our first date, I was relieved that none of them was in evidence. But then as we gained momentum all four of them leaped out of the bushes simultaneously, laughing nervously and shouting, "Good-bye, Mommie. Good-bye, Daddy." They were joined by the barking of two dogs, one born in Georgia and one born in Connecticut.

We were momentarily embarrassed into silence. "Is that send-off a good omen or a bad one?" I finally asked.

Elizabeth moved imperceptively closer to me on the brown plastic seat of the Ford wagon and put her small hand with the gracefully pointed fingers on my sleeve. "I guess that is up to us." That was the first of thousands of miles we were to ride side by side in many different cars. At that moment I felt again that stirring down deep in my gut.

The following Spring Jim Laney, later president of Emory University and then Ambassador to South Korea, invited me to Cincinnati where he was pastor of a small suburban church. He had worked with me when he was a student at Yale and wanted me to join him for preaching services every evening during Holy Week. I do not remember any spectacular results although I tried to preach like Peter and he tried to pray like Paul. I do remember a great windstorm which blew the corrugated roof off the carport adjacent to the bedroom where I slept in some parishioner's house. I thought it was Judgment Day.

I accepted Jim's invitation partly because I thought Cincinnati and Atlanta were near enough that I could stretch the travel allowance to visit Elizabeth in Georgia. Once or twice during that week Jim asked me if I were worried about something.

"No. Not at all. Why do you ask?"

"You just seem preoccupied," he replied.

"Preoccupied?" I countered.

"Yes. Or in a hurry. Like when you started to give the benediction instead of the offertory prayer. Are you in a hurry to get out of here?"

When he discovered I was going to Georgia instead of home I confessed that I was in a hurry. At least I was eager. I took a flight to Atlanta and then a Greyhound bus to the little college town near Macon where Elizabeth's father was a professor in a Baptist college.

As the bus came into town, I saw Elizabeth standing quite alone at the corner of the Court House Square where the bus discharged passengers. The Court House itself was almost hidden by the blooming camellias and dogwood. She looked beautiful standing there in a light green linen dress and pretty high heeled shoes. I hopped off the bus eager for at least a brief embrace, but she greeted me as though I were a stranger she had been asked to meet and transport to the college campus.

"Here's the car," she said, pointing to a nearly new Oldsmobile "88" four door sedan. "You can put your suitcase in the back seat." And off we went.

As we left the Court House Square and turned onto a side street, she turned to me, "Hi! It's good to see you. I'm relieved. I don't think anyone saw us."

"Oh," I said with a questioning bewilderment in my voice, "are you ashamed of your Yankee connections?"

"No. It's not that," Elizabeth replied without smiling, "I just don't want it in the newspaper that 'Mrs. Hinshaw, our sixth grade teacher, entertained a Connecticut widower over the Easter weekend.'"

Elizabeth's efforts to keep me more or less hidden were in vain. Southern Baptists hardly know when Lent is, but they do celebrate Easter after a fashion. There was no way to get out of going to church on Easter. So we went. Her father and mother and Leigh and Layton and Elizabeth and I. We were shown to a pew squarely in the middle of the congregation. Later, squarely in the middle of the service, the friendly minister said, "Professor and Mrs. Davis have a guest this weekend from Yale Divinity School. I wish he would stand and lead us in the Easter prayer."

I felt absolutely trapped. Elizabeth was quietly crimson and looked straight ahead. I had not prayed extemporaneously in public since . . . I don't know when. I want to phrase my prayers carefully. But I did pray extemporaneously that day. I even slipped in a little prayer for ecumenicity and the unity of Christ's church. I do not remember that anything was ever said to me about the content of my prayer, but there was a lot of bustling on the church steps afterwards around and about Professor Davis' guest!

Something else of importance happened that day. Professor Davis, I suspect, well knew that Elizabeth was serious about this Yankee minister-professor who believed in *infant* baptism, which Professor Davis pointed out was not Biblical! Elizabeth had reluctantly left the West Coast and returned to her parents' warm welcome in Georgia before Layton was born. Her father was delighted with a son at last. He had been the boy's father for almost ten years. He took him fishing, let him struggle happily with his clubs on the golf course, helped him build a house in the backyard for a homeless dog.

Concerned about Layton's eternal welfare as well as his temporal welfare, Professor Davis had taken all the appropriate steps to make sure that Layton, although a little young for it, was baptized by immersion that Easter Sunday in that Southern Baptist Church. It was a beautiful moment.

This baptism was not only a sign of God's love, it was also a sign of the protective and singular love that an older man had for a little boy. A love shown again in a few months when he encouraged his daughter, Elizabeth, to follow the bidding of her heart even if it meant he must give up that little boy to another man and another world. But Layton was baptized. Properly. A Southern Baptist saint of God had seen to that. And that was for keeps. *Ego baptizatus sum.*

CHAPTER 2

A Bow Is Set in the Cloud
A Promise Is Made

The next summer when we all ended up again in Maine, Elizabeth and I decided if we were going to marry, we had better do it fast while it still felt like a lark to the children and us. We did. We were married one afternoon in the village church. Professor Davis offered us the vows; the local minister made it official; his wife played the piano tentatively (by mistake she played the three hymns we had marked as the only ones we did not want to hear); Bob and Barbara Cushman, the matchmakers, were our attendants; Elizabeth's mother, some unexpected visitors, and our four children stood with us.

The wedding service was mostly a blur for me. I was troubled and anxious about many things and eager to get it over with. Curiously, about all I remember was how warm Professor Davis's large heavy hand was as he took mine and placed it in Elizabeth's. Her hand was clammy cold but not her eyes. They engaged mine steadily and her voice was clear and resolute: "I do promise and covenant, before God and these witnesses, to be your loving and faithful wife, in plenty and in want, in joy and in sorrow, in sickness and in health; until death we do part."

The promise was made.

There followed tea and cakes at the Davis cottage.

We started out on a brief honeymoon but soon had to stop and take out the rocks which the Cushman sons had enboldened and assisted our children to put in the hubcaps of the Ford wagon.

7

After two nights in Quebec, we came back to Maine, picked up the four children and went to a summer school for pastors in Deering, New Hampshire, where I was scheduled to teach for three weeks.

We were greeted there by my old friends, absolute strangers to Elizabeth. One was a Yale colleague who at that time was Holmes Professor of Old Testament Criticism and Interpretation. He claims that he did not participate in the decoration of the bridal suite, the most remote cabin on the property, with yards and yards of toilet paper. I was rather pleased by the riotous reception. It was not quite what Elizabeth had expected at a pastors' school.

Our honeymoon in that friendly place was not very private but it was lively and warm. Then one day, while carrying an overloaded basket, full of wet wash, up some steep New England farmhouse stairs, Elizabeth suffered an injury to her back. She was so quiet and uncomplaining about her injury that I could not believe it was truly serious. Finally, a local doctor, suspecting a fractured disc, urged hospitalization. Eventually the Cushmans came to visit and took the children back to the grandparents in Maine. I kept Elizabeth and the two dogs.

With the children safe in Maine, I made an ambulance of the station wagon, and the dogs and I took Elizabeth to New Haven and the Yale medical resources for diagnosis and immediate surgery. It was a low and lonely time for Elizabeth. It was years before I realized how hard it had been for her. I fear that her beloved cocker spaniel was her chief comforter in the hard months which followed. I was much too uptight about my own problems of adjustment to sense the total dislocation she was suffering, not so much from the surgery as from New Haven.

The grandparents kept the children for several weeks and Elizabeth was sent home from the hospital into my custody to complete her recovery from the surgery. While I cared for her I worked at getting the house ready for the enlarged family. It was a big house in central New Haven which I had purchased only months before. I was enthralled with the prospect of restoring it to its former glory. Elizabeth was eager to share in the project. It was she who suggested that we use some money her parents had given us as a wedding present to buy cherry red carpeting, which I passionately coveted, for the broad stairway with two turns and two landings which soared up out of the front entrance hall and was the chief architectural feature of this turn of the century house. Eventually we did just that. It made for an impressive entrance largely lost to most of the family who filled its broad spaces with overshoes or volley balls according to the season.

But that roomy house was not all sweeping stairways and cherry carpets. The cellar was a mess. The former owner, an old man befuddled by loneliness and housekeeping, had actually left the dirty dishes from his last breakfast for me to deal with when I took possession of the house. He was off to Florida. The cellar reflected the same weary state of mind and body. Newspapers were stacked to the ceiling and sacks full of bottles had been there long enough to have cellar dust settled deep inside them. The long unused laundry tubs were almost hidden underneath the rotting garden hoses and the soil-encrusted dahlia stakes and the chicken fencing someone had stacked on the smooth gray soapstone of the twin tubs.

Ever since I had moved into that old house the cellar had called me but had won no response. Affairs of the heart as well as less exciting academic responsibilities had kept me out of the cellar. But I knew when the kids rejoined us and Elizabeth's possessions arrived from Georgia we would need the space. So while Elizabeth recuperated, I cleaned out the cellar and made endless trips to the New Haven dump in the burdened station wagon. I found the cellar a safe place, a refuge from the new responsibilities I had taken on, a shelter from the pain in a new relationship which sometimes was more evident than its pleasure.

It was not far to the dump, and Elizabeth's first outings were those trips. She insisted that the dogs go with us even though they climbed all over her with wet affection. The dogs had developed tolerance for each other but, like the children, had discovered some aspects of this new domestic situation which undercut former privileges. In such blended families always one youngest child and one oldest is displaced, but that is only the beginning! The dogs, too, had to adjust to some changes they didn't exactly favor. Elizabeth had only one lap. She always offered it freely to animals and children alike, but there was only room for one. The dogs made the best of it. It was on those trips to the dump that we learned that the rest of the family, including us, would have to catch up with the dogs if our marriage were to survive.

In retrospect, I wonder if it was not then that we really began to get acquainted. The earliest stage of love's unfolding had been clear to us since that first moment on the beach, but "philia," friendship love, had been smothered by practical urgencies, over-looked and neglected. Single parents seek not only new lovers but a father or a mother for children whose welfare is upper-most in their lives. I suspect that we had been overly preoccu-pied with concern for the children. We had romantic ideas about this new enlarged combined family. We thought that our good intentions were enough to make it just happen. Such a lot of unrealistic hogwash. It all rested on the health and strength of our relationship, the quality of our friendship, yet we scarcely knew one another. It was almost like an arranged marriage. We knew we shared common values and believed we shared a com-mon culture. We were mostly right about the values; we were mostly wrong about the culture!

Blending one family out of two is extremely difficult under the best of circumstances, but blending North and South, urban and rural, Southern Baptist and New England Congregational, that is another matter. Talk about conflict! We didn't even share the same tools and language for battle!

Elizabeth had been teaching sixth grade in a small Georgia town. She was accustomed to a telephone system with a live op-erator who would look out her window to answer inquiries about the arrival or departure of the bus for Atlanta. Elizabeth had shopped in stores around the Court House square where every other clerk had gone to school with her or to her. She had at-tended Baptist churches all her life where Baptists outranked even the Episcopalians for community prestige. She had taught in a school system where the teachers were required to visit in the homes of the children they taught every year. Connecticut was not Georgia.

We had dial telephones and express trains to Grand Central and child psychiatrists by the dozen. I had been accustomed to a housekeeper who never asked me to take any responsibility around the house and only seldom for the children. She never called for help unless the plumbing was backing up or the roof was on fire. She was a remarkable woman, Marion Easton, who had seen my desperate ad for a housekeeper in *The Christian Science Monitor* and answered it. She was on the faculty of the Boston School of Occupational Therapy but had long wanted to cook and care for children. So she took a leave of absence to try her hand at very demanding work in a very troubled house. Un-sung heroines!

I only had to tell her I would be away for a weekend, taking my place in the procession of ordained professors who preached in New England colleges where chapel attendance was still required and cleverness in the pulpit was a greater asset than piety, and she would plan something for the children. It was quite different one time that first year of our marriage when I told Elizabeth I would be away, unexpectedly, for a Saturday night and Sunday.

She simply went into orbit!

"And what am I supposed to do?" she shouted at me. "Scrub the kitchen floor?"

"I'm sorry," I said, in helpless surprise.

"Sorry, sorry, sorry," she retorted. "You're always sorry. But I'm the one who stays home."

"But we need the money," I countered.

"Sure. And you need the escape," she whispered angrily as she went out the back door to find some comfort in the little herb garden she had tried to protect all summer and fall.

Such explosions were few and far between. But even one was one too many for me. I had been reared in the shadow of a family behavior system which made no room for the expression of negative feelings and which confused anger with hatred. It was fortunate for me that Elizabeth had not been hindered by any such restraint on the expression of feeling. Without such venting I do not think she could have kept her promise; except she did seem curiously connected to God with whom she appeared to be on very good and intimate terms.

We both tried very hard to meet each other's need and to be sensitive to the dislocation the children were suffering. In response to a magazine article on child rearing and out of a sense of duty, I tried to give Elizabeth time off and "do things" myself with the children. But I was never much good at it. When I complained to a family counsellor, whom we consulted, about what a chore it was, she suggested that I find things to do with them that I, too, would enjoy. It seems in retrospect that all we did together after that was to visit used car lots or eat fried clams at Howard Johnson's.

As that first year moved along, New Haven tried to be hospitable to Elizabeth and she made one or two good friends in our three years there, but none close enough to know about the miscarriage she suffered or help her with her feeling that Southern Baptists were a large ecclesiastical joke at Yale Divinity School.

New Haven was as provincial in its own high-hatted way as any southern town. My friends there appeared as innocent as I about the strain this new world placed on Elizabeth.

She bears some responsibility that her new acquaintances never learned she was a pioneer environmentalist. She and her first husband, graduates of Rollins College, had spent an experimental period of self-subsistence on an island in Puget Sound. It was there she had become a skilled animal and bird scatologist and an expert with bow and rifle. In the 1950's these skills did not win interest at university cocktail parties.

Elizabeth was not very comfortable at those parties discussing existentialism and exchanging reactions to the latest issue of the *Kenyon Review*. They were threatening to both of us but I had more confidence in my finesse than in her candor, and I was more relaxed alone than when I felt I had responsibility to run interference for Elizabeth also. Some social occasions were so uncomfortable for us that I devised an "urgent trip" to Colorado to avoid the president's formal dinner party for newly tenured professors. Now, more than thirty years later, Elizabeth would be a celebrity in such circles if, by some happy accident, it became known that she had had extensive "hands on" experience in wildlife management. But you can be sure she would not volunteer that information. It felt embarrassingly out-of-place in the New Haven social scene of the 50's.

I do not believe our marriage would have survived the New Haven years if it had not been for Elizabeth's powerful sense of commitment. There simply was no tolerable alternative for her. A promise is a promise. The survival of our marriage was also helped by those wonderful trips to the New Haven City dump which we continued regularly, trips on which none of the children was ever invited and the dogs were never excluded. For the truth is that I had no idea of the depth of the pain Elizabeth was suffering. The fractured disc was nothing to the fracture of her life caused by our marriage and by all the consequences.

She missed the friendly small community, she missed her sixth graders who adored her, and after the surgery she missed the energy she had always enjoyed. She also missed the less formal worship services of her church and the gospel songs they sang in Georgia, strong on personal relationship with Jesus Christ, songs which sometimes were taken with amused disdain in divinity school circles.

One evening when a divinity school crowd was having fun around our piano at the expense of some of the simple and tuneful songs of youth encampments and revival services, I noticed that Elizabeth quietly left the room. "Blessed Assurance" and "What A Friend We Have in Jesus" were not songs to be fooled with. She retreated up the cherry carpet toward the privacy of our bedroom as the happy party jazzed up "Standing on the Promises of God."

She really takes those songs seriously, I thought with amazement as I noted her escape from the party. Surely they don't still sing them in the Rollins Chapel! All at once I was drawn down into an airless pit of despair from which I saw no escape. It was suddenly clear to me that Elizabeth and I were world's apart. I was confronted by the dreadful truth that among my New Haven friends I was often embarrassed by her. What a devastating, guilt-ridden acknowledgment.

* * * * * * * *

By the mysterious provision of a hidden Providence we still needed to make many more trips to the New Haven city dump. Locked up in the station wagon with the dogs crawling over us and the wagon jammed full with junk we had to be rid of to make the house livable, our sub-conscience selves apparently could not avoid the urgency of the symbolism. There was a lot of junk from the past in our lives we needed to get off our backs. Some of it we could dispose of ourselves, but there was much, mostly unspoken between us, that needed Someone else to take it on. "Forgiveness releases us from the irreversibility of the past." We came to believe that a trip to the dump should be part of every anniversary celebration for married couples and other committed friends. Can "agape" then be far away?

Certainly, it was on those trips back and forth to the New Haven dump that we began to be significant friends. It was our "engagement" period, that time when couples once really got acquainted before they made life-long promises, the time when "philia" love began to emerge to enhance "erotic" love. Together we began to face the horrendous reality of what we had done and began to understand what we must do to make this marriage of two disparate families, with two communication systems, two cultures, work.

I felt the chances of success were very slim. This new world was so strange and demanding and uncomfortable that I, like the Israelites, wanted to go back to Egypt, return to the comfortable and free life I had experienced as a widower with a good house-keeper. Somehow this new large ideal family wasn't what I had expected.

The children, too, were not totally content. It was harder for some of them than others, but it was a new world of misery as well as miracle for each of them. It involved compromises and changes they hadn't anticipated. Where would we celebrate Christmas? Who would get to put the angel on the top of the tree? Who would get to ride in the front seat whenever he or she wished? Who was this new sister or brother who had pushed in between my mother or my father and me? So this new large ideal family wasn't quite what they had expected either. There were many days when they, weeping, would also have gladly run back to Egypt.

But Elizabeth? It certainly wasn't what she had bargained for. New Haven was not the new Jerusalem. But there was no way she was going to turn tail and find refuge in Egypt or Georgia either one. It was many years before I understood what kept her so resolute as the family and personal problems multiplied. Our future was already secured, she believed. It was not up for grabs. It had been secured by a bow set in a New England cloud, our promises before God and God's to us. At least Elizabeth's God!

I mightily wish we had known then what we learned in retirement: the crucial difference between expectations and possibilities. How often our expectations in life, vocational, romantic, practical, block our possibilities. If we have always expected to be a lawyer or a farmer, we may never open ourselves to be discovered by impressive gifts we have to become something very different from a lawyer or a farmer. We have to put aside our expectations and open ourselves up to our possibilities.

When bitter circumstances compelled Elizabeth and me to relinquish some of our expectations, leave them at the dump with less attractive junk, then a whole new world of possibilities for this new but troubled marriage and family began to speak up and demand our nurturing attention. In facing that disappointment honestly, our love began to grow beyond the passion which fueled it and gave it excitement. We came to trust one another as friends. On those ritual trips to the New Haven dump our relationship began to deepen and find roots to sustain us. We were enabled to be open to some specific possibilities beyond the tenured security of Yale and the expectation of long summers in Maine and sabbatic renewals every seven years. Those possibilities summoned us to California.

We had been married three years when I accepted a call to be a parish minister again. This time in Berkeley, 1960. Elizabeth protested that she had not married a professor to become a minister's wife, and besides, she argued, we could never sell a beautiful but strange brick and glass house we had just built. But once we visited California nothing could keep us in New Haven, not even that brand new house, designed without a linen closet by a distinguished Chinese architect and built without a linen closet by an exacting Scandinavian contractor.

The house was an expensive project we had undertaken to give our new family a common experience and shared ownership of our environment, to help us live up to our expectations of a happy university family. Now the opportunity came to move all of us together to a place and people none of us knew. Here were possibilities we never dreamed of demanding our attention. Urgent emergency 'trips to the dump' to reflect on those possibilities saved us from allowing old expectations to kill them.

Our oldest child, Leigh, now almost seventeen, would be a senior in high school when we arrived in Berkeley and the younger three would represent us in each of the three grades of junior high. It appeared a very foolish time to make such a move, but it was clear to both Elizabeth and me that it was the right thing to do. The unfolding possibilities felt more full of grace and joy than our most reasonable expectations. So we packed up and moved. Not only furniture and china, but dogs and cats and hampsters and a potted palm and a battered buoy from the coast of Maine.

When we reached Reno on that hot summer crossing of the continent, the four children came to our motel room and demanded an audience. The next day we would arrive in Berkeley. Was there any need, they asked, that the people in Berkeley had to know that we had been two families? Elizabeth's children had already chosen to take my name and the legalities of that change had long since been completed. We agreed that we couldn't lie about our double history but we didn't need to make a big thing out of it. So it was that we drove into Berkeley with a fresh sense of unity and wholeness.

I am sure that the trips Elizabeth and I made to the New Haven dump in the first years of our marriage were a crucial element working for that pleasant outcome. Our experience in those years confirmed for us Norman Cousin's observation that marriage is an "adventure in forgiveness." But there was something else working for us silently and powerfully: I think Elizabeth must have kept her eye on that bow in the New England cloud and prayed a lot . . . in private, rooted as she was in the promise she had made. Not so with me. I only prayed in public. With carefully chosen language. The God whom Elizabeth knew apparently wasn't much put off by split infinitives or rollicking tunes.

CHAPTER 3

Taken Away to Die in the Wilderness?

After seventeen years in Berkeley we picked up our furniture and china once again and moved across the San Francisco Bay to San Anselmo. Then six years later I reached retirement there at the San Francisco Theological Seminary and once again we picked up the furniture and china and moved. Once more we needed a first class dump.

Our parents were all dead, our children all grown, and we were ready to fit ourselves and our dogs and cats and plants and some of our furniture and china into a small house we loved in the wine country seventy miles north of the Bay. We had bought this house early in our California years. It is secreted in Knights Valley, a choice and fertile land beyond the last ridge of the much busier Napa Valley. We had spent every possible holiday fixing it up and after much deliberation decided to make it the base for our active retirement. At long last we were free to do exactly that. We could hardly wait to get settled there and begin our adventures far and wide.

We moved in June.

At breakfast one morning in mid-August Elizabeth said to me, "You really must do something about the patio."

I looked out. There was the patio. Beyond it were the vineyards and an uninterrupted view of Mt. St. Helena, the highest mountain in this part of California. Sometimes in the winter it has a dusting of snow on its peaks and everyone is very excited,

17

asking John at the post office or Darrin at the Shell station, "Did you see the snow this morning?" In the summer the mountain is inhospitable with the dark patches of forest choked all around with crackle-brown grass. More than once we have watched its massive shoulders burn and we have applauded in the heat from our patio as pilots have aimed the bellies of their planes, filled with powdery yellow flame retardant, at some blazing center.

On that very hot August morning, Mt. St. Helena could have had both snow and fire on it for all anyone could tell from our breakfast table looking across the wide patio. It was stacked high: tables, chests, a spool bed with chipped green paint, two double bed mattresses, one set of bedsprings, a croquet set with the wire wickets tied to the broken box which held seven balls, a collection of lamps with lampshades falling around their feet like "covering" skirts, a ping pong table loaded with all the seconds we had of toasters, fireplace tools, laundry hampers, grass clippers, a green metal typewriter table missing one caster and *three* davenports . . . and much more.

"You really must do something about it," Elizabeth said again.

"It won't rain for another couple of months."

"Call the Salvation Army."

"We can't give all that good stuff away."

"We are not going to have another garage sale."

"What then do you propose?"

Elizabeth had no new proposal . . . not just then!

To say that "we moved" does not do justice to the experience. We had moved before. We had picked up our accumulations and moved them from one house to another as our resident family grew smaller. We had moved from Berkeley to San Anselmo. Also we never forgot that once we had moved across the nation in July in an station wagon without air conditioning with four adolescent children, two dogs, a cat who had kittens en route, several turtles and a couple of productive hampsters. From New England to California in July. That is moving!

But this was different. We were moving to a small farmhouse from a city house conceived and built in a more civilized time, with an attic and a basement and a "spare room" and lots of bookshelves. But there was another problem. The farmhouse was already full of furniture. The stuff there, for the most part duplicates of what we were bringing from San Anselmo, was of no great value, but it was the stuff of our childhood. Absurdly, we came to retirement with four davenports!

We each had one when we got married. We inherited one when my mother died as no one else had room for it and at that time no one could bear to give the old family piece away. Then we bought a new one upholstered in velour to add a little class to the Dean's residence which we had to furnish when we moved to the seminary campus. This final move to the country was a moment of truth for those davenports and for much else.

Elizabeth and I finally agreed on a fast and easy solution to the problem posed by our piles of tired possessions. We would give the stuff away. What no one else wanted we would take to the dump. So it ended up with the Salvation Army and a number of other worthy enterprises sending a truck with a driver and a usually wordless assistant to haul away what they wanted. I should not say it "ended up" that way. That was only the beginning of the "ending up."

Actually it ended up with Elizabeth and me and our two dogs holding a requiem at the county dump. Unless the New Haven city dump has improved a lot since the summer of 1957, it doesn't compare with the Sonoma County dump. Northern California simply excells at everything! That county dump, until it was converted into a "land fill transfer point," was lovely. It commanded a high point of land overlooking scattered farmhouses and a distant ribbon of landscaped freeway. The gulls there cawed in harmony and seemed to share the bounty graciously. The wind always wafted the smell away from the visitors and even the attendant in the little cabin at the gate was polite when he or she extracted from you the modest fee.

We had been very quiet as we drove up our valley to the Sonoma County dump. It felt as though we had converted our old half-ton truck into a hearse and crowded the mourners into the cab. Over the previous weekend hardhearted friends had helped me load the truck with everything that we couldn't give away. They had insisted on doing most of the lifting in order to spare my tricky back. They were sure I would have no trouble unloading it at the dump without undue strain. Just pull it off and let it fly, they said. That airy attitude failed to take into consideration our attachment to some of this stuff, especially my dear deceased mother's great davenport with its tattered dark upholstery. I could stretch my full six feet out on it flat with room to spare at head and foot. How could I ever "just pull it off and let it fly"?

Usually our frequent trips to the dump were happy celebrations. They provoked poignant recollections of important chapters in our private history as a couple. We never forgot the hours in the New Haven dump and once laughingly celebrated an anniversary in Australia by having a friend take us to the dump in Adelaide.

So here we were, heading out together for a visit to another dump. The rays of the sun bounced off the yellow brown hot humps of hillside along the winding country road and multiplied the heat through the windshield. The adoptive descendents of the Georgia dog and the Connecticut dog were crowded with us in the cab of our wonderfully beat-up truck. The toll of the years showed as Elizabeth absently stroked the dog whose head was on her lap. Her lovely, vigorous hands were twisted all out of shape by arthritis. The dog looked so content with her stroking that I sensed he enjoyed, as I did, the warm soothing surprising smoothness of those tortured hands. They felt like exceedingly fine velvet. We did not say much. It was growing very hot. Heat and Elizabeth were not good friends. I was glad that this ancient truck with its prized and powerful 350 cubic inch engine, given to us by one of my nephews when I retired, was equipped with air conditioning which a resourceful mechanic had managed to get working again.

If I had not long since learned that Elizabeth credited the trips to the New Haven dump with saving our marriage and that as a consequence she had deep romantic associations with dumps, any dump, I would think she had gone along with me on *this* trip solely in order to be sure that the truck came back empty. Well, it did. But it was hard. It was hard at the dump that day. It was especially wrenching to realize what I had done as I looked down into the stinking fascinating depths of the Sonoma County dump and saw my mother's aged and damaged davenport, rejected even by the Salvation Army, and now by us, angled upward toward us as though to say, You can still pull me back if you will.

"Change and decay in all around I see," I thought.

But I said to Elizabeth and the dogs as we stood there behind the truck at the edge of the dump, "I read all the *Bobbsey Twins* stretched out on that sofa."

Elizabeth turned slowly and looked at me.

"And *Gulliver's Travels*," I continued.

She looked again hardly turning her head.

"And *War and Peace*."

The dogs didn't say anything and they didn't turn their heads either until the monster crunching smashing pushing-around machine swept up mother's sofa into the rolling mass of old wallboard and grass clippings and pickle jars and splintered boards black with rot. It was the only piece of furniture on which the dogs had ever been allowed to sleep unmolested. I thought one of them cried a little.

When we were well out of the dump and back on the highway headed home and the dogs had settled down between us, Elizabeth spoke: "You really didn't need to be so dramatic . . . and so drastic with the sofa. I'm sure somebody would have loved to have the frame anyway."

I didn't say a word.

After a moment, she said, "What do you want for lunch?"

Too late, little lady, too late, I thought, still mulling over the sofa. Why didn't you offer such a compromise earlier. I could have kept it in the garage for afternoon naps.

"Whatever you've got," I finally said. "Hot dogs. Chicken soup. I'm not fussy."

The next morning I got out of bed, walked over to the closet and started to take off my pajamas. I dropped the pants to the floor and tried to step out of them. My right foot got snared in the limp pile of pajama legs and I reached down to disentangle it and hang the resisting garment in the closet. Wham! My back! It was as though the massive machine which I had watched compact the stuff at the dump had compacted my spine and rib cage. I let out an involuntary gasp and caught myself with one hand on the frame of the closet door.

"Is it your back again?" Elizabeth was alarmed.

I nodded "yes," reluctantly confessing another betrayal by my back, for which I always have felt personally and morally responsible.

"Get flat," she said as she hurried out of her side of the bed.

"I can't move," I whispered.

Hobbled by the pajama bottoms and bent over like some child positioned for punishment, with Elizabeth's encouragement and guidance I inched back, inch-by-pain-streaked inch to the edge of the bed. I eased back on to it in a sitting position so close to the edge that it was only by grace I didn't fall to the floor. With incredible patience, Elizabeth, with her virtually graspless hands, gently held me and encouraged me and finally eased me flat on the bed I had just left. She covered up my nakedness and then just stood there and looked at me. I thought I heard a whispered opinion about mother's davenport. But I have never asked her. More likely she was thinking, as was I, that we should have moved to an adult community with guaranteed life care after all. Had we been taken away to die in the wilderness?

She did say, "And we don't know a doctor within seventy miles."

CHAPTER 4

"Is There No Balm in Gilead;
Is There No Physician There?"

Everything about our plan to live in the country and remain in an age-integrated natural community was fine except the question of health care. During all our years in California we had been within a few minutes of one of the finest medical centers in the country. Elizabeth had been under the care of a noted arthritis specialist who, though he never knew her by name from one appointment to the next, was medically "the best." There was even a skilled orthopedist, who did know my name because he was a warm and caring person and because I was his mother's pastor. He had seen my back in spasm several times. For Americans who love specialists and demand top medical care, we had been beautifully situated. What romantic nonsense persuaded us to move out to the sticks.

Now, here we were six miles from a little town that doesn't even have a dry cleaner or a shoe repair shop, 25 miles from a small city, Santa Rosa, which can hardly support a junior college much less a medical school, and 70 miles from home, the famed San Francisco Bay Area, with hospitals and doctors with world-wide reputations.

As I began to relax just a little on the bed, I was forcefully reminded why I had got out of bed that morning in the first place.

"Elizabeth," I whispered, "I have to pee."

23

"You do?" she responded, as though that was simply not a possibility.

"Do we have a urinal anymore?" I asked.

"I have no idea where it is."

"No matter. I think I may have to have the bed pan."

"I don't know where that is either."

"It's in an orange crate in your closet," I said. "I saw it yesterday when I was hunting some band-aids."

Elizabeth found it, removed the bathroom supplies stored in it for moving, and brought it to the bed.

"I can't get up on that."

"Well, you will have to . . . or mess up the bed. Can you roll over on your side? Then I'll put it in the bed and you roll back on to it."

"I don't think I can do it."

"Well, try, anyway."

Gradually this plan worked. Much to my relief, I might add. Then I called Elizabeth who had gone to make some coffee to come get the bed pan. I really had only needed a urinal. Elizabeth was barely five feet tall and seldom weighed over 115 pounds. There was no way I could lift myself up off that pan so she could pull it out; and there was no way she could pull it out with any of my weight still on it. She had very little strength in either of her hands. She thought archeologists are going to be puzzled when they find all her plastic knuckles, the result of unsatisfactory hand surgery.

Actually, the pan somehow gave my back support so it wasn't too uncomfortable and the one old codeine tablet we had found was beginning to have some effect. So, out of necessity, we just left the pan there, unpleasant as that was, while we figured out what to do about my back. Finally we decided that the only real option we had was to call a young doctor who had recently come to the little town down the road, Calistoga, a place known more for its mud baths and wineries than for its medical facilities. We weren't very hopeful about a physician who would settle down in a town of three or four thousand people.

Elizabeth reached his answering service. It was still only breakfast time. Within ten minutes he called back from the Community Hospital in the little city 25 miles away which has a junior college. Elizabeth reported with surprise and relief that he said he would stop by on his way home from the hospital. He shouldn't be too long.

A house call? I thought. A house call on a patient he had never seen before? Either he doesn't have much to do or isn't very particular. I found scant comfort in either speculation. We had not had much experience with physicians who made housecalls. I had had several other episodes of a similar back problem. One time, eight years earlier, the constriction was so severe that my abdomen swelled up so it looked like I needed an obstetrician more than an orthopedist. On that occasion, right from the bed, I telephoned Tom, our orthopedist friend, who had seen me before and whose aged but vigorous mother was in my pastoral care. He prescribed some pills which Elizabeth went and got. But they weren't too effective. So several hours later I called him again. I thought he would stop by and take a look on his way home. I knew he felt I had been very understanding of his mother who had strong convictions about her funeral, an event the impatient lady felt was being indecently postponed.

When Tom finally returned my call he said that if the pills he had previously prescribed did not help, he could only help me more if I got myself down to the emergency room at the hospital.

"I can't possibly do that, Tom. I can hardly hold the phone."

"Then you could call the ambulance."

No way, I thought, remembering when Elizabeth's father had died in another upstairs bedroom in that house. The undertaker and his helpers had had to hold the gurney almost upright to manage the turn in the narrow stairway. I had watched in horror for fear they would lose the body in the process.

"I can't do that either, Tom," I said. "Maybe if I hang on a while longer, the pills will get to work."

"I think they may," he replied. "If not, I'll come as soon as I have a break. I'm on call."

"By the way, Tom," I managed sarcastically, "when you call me that your mother is dying, I'll have you bring her down to my study at the church."

I was sick enough to be delighted that for once I had made the smart reply which usually falls into that category of replies you think of later and only wish you had been quick enough to say. Much later you are glad you didn't. It had no effect on Tom. He was a friend! He knew I wasn't usually difficult.

So on that August morning Elizabeth and I fell quiet as we waited for this strange physcian who was our only hope of the moment. It felt like a very long time to me, perched on that bed pan, before I heard the gravel in our driveway announce the approach of a car. So it was for the first time this small town family physician, who has a *summa cum laude* certificate hanging among the credentials on his office wall, turned his well-worn modest German-made sedan into our driveway. He had come as he said he would. Elizabeth ushered him into our bedroom. A slender young man with steel rimmed eye glasses, he seemed to be taking it all in at once, us and the room and Abby, the cat, on the bed.

It never occurred to me that he was probably younger than our youngest son, not yet forty. He was "the doctor" and at the moment all the mystique built up around physicians in our culture surrounded him. Now we didn't need to worry or make decisions. The doctor had come. He would tell us what to do.

"What's the problem?"

I began to describe my symptoms.

"No," he said. "I mean. Are you propped up to help your back or do you normally rest arched up like that?"

I began to see myself enthroned on the bed pan with the sheet falling around me like a royal tent. Elizabeth began to laugh. She started to explain, "It's the . . . . " But the sight of me and the cat and the hidden bed pan was more than she could explain without laughing.

I was annoyed by her laughter. I realized that I was a strange sight piled up on that bed like a bundle of sheets on the way to the laundry. Somehow in that moment I felt stuck, not just on the bed pan, but in abject helplessness. Maybe this experience symbolized my years of jealousy and quarrels with the medical profession. This strange young man had all the power. He stood over me with youthfulness and professional skill. Probably there was an expensive car out in the driveway, the sort I would lust after. I lay there powerless. Do with me as you please and then send me an unnegotiated bill.

In retrospect, knowing a lot more about the draining struggle of primary physicians in the changing medical scene and respecting and loving this particular doctor very much, I wonder how I could have had such a surge of anger. Is it a clue to how the powerless in our society feel? Does it help a privileged person like me to enter into the experience of those who never can "call the shots," so they shoot at anything they can? This loss of power characterizes life increasingly as one grows older.

How can one deal with it? Is there some mystical graffiti the old can scratch at night on the steamy urine-smelling walls of the nursing home? How else can they make common cause with the other powerless in society? With money they are not quite powerless. Perhaps it is not the money but the powerlessness which drives them into segregated adult communities. There, at least, the playing field levels off! What else can they do with any kind of grace and style but play and laugh. So I laughed. At myself. It's no solution, but it helps. It helps you keep your dignity and your relationship to others, even to the powerful, like this young man standing over me. Maybe it can cover your anger and your hopelessness and your sorrow and your privacy. So I laughed.

Dr. Mueller pulled back the sheet. Quite exposed. Like my mother at ninety whom the cheery nurse insisted on calling by her first name. Not even her best friends did that. Mother played dead until the nurse followed my suggestion and called her Mrs. Barr. Then she chose to respond. That was all the power she had left!

"I'm stuck," I said.

"So I see." Then he smiled easily. With two strong hands he carefully lifted my weight off the pan and indicated to Elizabeth that she could have the pan now if she still wanted it. Then he let me down very gently.

So we were introduced to Francis L. Mueller, M.D.

CHAPTER 5

Some Have Compassion, Making a Difference

During undergraduate days at Grinnell College I had seriously considered going to medical school. I convinced myself that as a doctor I could care for people, be socially useful, and get rich at the same time. But there were two factors that worked against it. The first was a college course in organic chemistry. I couldn't even finish it! The second was a strange episode one summer in a remote mountain community where I ended up acting as a midwife while the father got drunk in one corner of the room which was his family's entire residence—except for a tiny annex out beyond the back door.

Brash, naive, and twenty-one, I didn't know anything about birthing. I hardly knew where babies came from. But caught up in this crisis, I was not one to admit my inexperience. The mother, with her baby half born, was in no position to be choosy about help. I had gone there to visit the barber, her husband, who operated out of a room facing the street and housed his family in the single room behind. He was far too drunk to cut my hair but sober enough to take me into the back room where his wife, deep in labor, needed some help. This country woman gave me curt instructions as the three of us, the mother, the baby and I, finished up what she and her boorish husband had started.

After it was all over and I, between swellings of nausea, had carefully cleaned up the newborn, the mother stood up, rolled up the soaked and bloody newspapers off the bed and called across the room to her husband, "Get up, Pinkie, you drunken bastard, and come over here and help me make up this bed."

Then she turned to me. I had just put the baby down in a brown cardboard crib she had improvised. It had stenciled letters on one end, "Campbell's Tomato." The thought of thick tomato soup almost finished my usefulness. My last meal was still bubbling behind my tonsils. "As for you, sonny boy," she said, "you can just get the hell out of here." I thought that was a good idea.

I suppose it is just as well for everyone in general that I got the hell out of there and turned my back forever on a career in medicine. Many times when making pastoral calls in a hospital I have wondered about my earlier dreams of being a physician. I have never forgotten one time when I was visiting a parishioner who had had early open heart surgery at Presbyterian Hospital in San Francisco. He insisted on pulling up his hospital gown and showing me the freshly sewed up incision which seemed to me to reach from his navel to his chin and back down around both his armpits. He wanted me to be duly appreciative. Just a quick glance didn't satisfy him. He traced his fingers slowly up and down and around the incisions as he gave a personal illustrated lecture. As my head got lighter and lighter, I finally managed to have a severe coughing fit which took me quickly out into the corridor.

I found easier ways than being a doctor to participate in our materialistic society and own the convertibles and station wagons and pickups and antique limousines that have been my weakness all my life. Buy them second hand! or better still, marry widows, which I have done twice, and each of them came to the altar with a better car than I had ever owned! Elizabeth long claimed that I married her for her 1955 Oldsmobile "Rocket 88."

Now Elizabeth was not thinking about automobiles but about me and my back and our isolation and this young man who had come to help us. With the bedpan out of the way Dr. Mueller examined me carefully, asked a few questions, and then helped me get adjusted a little more comfortably in the bed.

"May I use your phone?" he asked.

"Surely," Elizabeth responded, getting up from the chair beside the bed where she had watched everything Mueller did and helped me answer his questions. "It's right through this door in the kitchen. Over there beyond the stove." Then she came back into the room. She was still in her housecoat.

"You've never had anything to eat," I said.

"That's all right. I've had my coffee. That's all I need."

"You can't live on coffee," I said with concern.

"You'd be surprised." With that she sat down in the chair beside the bed. "I know I shouldn't get so upset when you are ill. But my world just flies apart. Do you suppose it is because I love you so much . . . or is it that I am so dependent upon you?"

She put her hand on mine, the one that was almost folded shut with arthritis. "I can't even hold your hand anymore," she said.

"O yes, you can," I replied. "Here take my finger. I love to feel how soft your skin is. All hidden away in your hand." With that I put my finger into her hidden palm and we just looked at each other.

"Thank you," she said very privately. "That's nice."

We were very still for a while.

"Are you able to move a little now?" she asked after a time.

"Yes. I can get my breath, too. I guess that old codeine pill still had some punch."

"I like this young man," Elizabeth half whispered.

"Who do you suppose he's calling?" I said.

"He's probably letting his office know where he is," Elizabeth suggested.

"He'd better get a car phone if he makes many calls out in the country like this."

"Please don't heckle him," she whispered.

"I haven't heckled him."

"No. But you almost have."

Just as Elizabeth said that, Dr. Mueller returned.

"We were talking about your coming here, making a house call—especially on a stranger. Isn't that pretty uncommon today?" I asked.

Dr. Mueller looked up at me without saying a word as though he were waiting for me to go on while he continued thinking about something else, presumably me. A little silence didn't seem to bother this young man. It made me very nervous. A few straying strands of his straight sandy hair fell down and rested inside the top of his wire-rimmed eyeglasses. I wished he would brush his hair out of his eyes.

"When you said Dr. Hedin suggested me, I decided I'd better come. I don't know him personally, but he's highly regarded by the fraternity."

"The *fraternity*?" I raised my eyebrows.

"Don't worry. I'm no sexist. My partner is a woman. Better doc than I. Are you more comfortable now?" he asked.

"Elizabeth helped me move when you were on the phone. I think that old codiene must be OK."

"Do you have some more?" he asked Elizabeth.

"I think there are two or three left."

"Give him another in a couple of hours. I'll give you a prescription for pain and a relaxant before I go."

"We really do appreciate your coming," Elizabeth responded. "I'll come to town this afternoon for the prescriptions. It will be fun to tell Dr. Hedin how you rescued us."

"I'm not sure I remember him," Dr. Mueller said

"Well, you must have made an impression on him," Elizabeth replied. "He told us he had met you at some sort of meeting and suggested that we might get in touch with you. We hadn't planned on meeting you so soon."

This conversation between the two continued for a while, going on over me prostrate on the bed beneath them. Mueller was managing to learn quite a lot about us, about me! In an instant I thought this is what disabled people get so upset about, talking about them, in their presence, to a third party as though they were incompetent or voiceless. I felt Mueller was getting ready to leave and I guess I wanted to participate in whatever time we had left with him. The power issue again! Is this the ailment of age, I wondered, or my private personality perversity?

"I am really curious about the housecalls," I said in a surprisingly weak voice. "I can't remember a doctor coming into our house since I was a kid. Certainly not since Elizabeth and I have been married."

"Oh no, that's not fair," Elizabeth spoke up before I could do any more damage. "Tom Barber offered to come and Goggio came once. To the house on Ashby Avenue when father died."

"He only came to fill out the death certificate," I said with an edge of scorn.

"He came to comfort Mother," Elizabeth retorted. "You are mean."

"Your father died in your home?" It was Mueller. He was getting a family history without asking for it. But I thought we would probably pay for it!

"Yes. He and my mother were with us when he was diagnosed with leukemia. Dr. Goggio arranged for therapy at the Lawrence Radiation Lab. Goggio was excellent and kept a close eye on him. Father couldn't have gotten care like that at home in Georgia. Unless maybe at Emory in Atlanta. But that was too far. They lived with us until he died."

"That must have been a big change for them," Mueller suggested. "Georgia versus Berkeley?"

"It was better than their being alone. I suspect they were glad they really had no choice. After my father died my mother divided her time between us and my sister's in Tallapoosa, Georgia."

"Tallapoosa?" Mueller asked as though it were not quite possible.

"Yes, Tallapoosa. It's Indian I guess which is more than you can say for Calistoga, named by a drunken Mormon."

"So I have heard," said Mueller. "The 'Calistoga of Sarifonia'."

"Well, anyway," Elizabeth continued, "I hardly know which she liked better, Tallapoosa or Berkeley. There was political intrigue in both places. Only in Tallapoosa it had more to do with local issues like town officials stealing from an oil line or a distillery, both hidden in the woods. I was always jealous of my sister. I thought mother preferred to be with her. Later I learned my sister was jealous of me for the same reason. We laughed at mother's gift of making us both want her."

"Elizabeth's mother was good company," I added. "She read everything and nearly exhausted herself trying to keep out of our way. She said she loved both places but that it was a nuisance to have to change her politics and her religion every six months when she crossed the Mississippi. But come now, doctor, what about the housecalls?"

"You're hitting me at a tender place. I like to make housecalls because I think they are important. But there's some crucial equipment you need to practice good medicine, stuff you can't carry around in a bag. So you need the patient in the office or hospital."

"Of course," I countered, "but it seems to me that there are some things you need to know about the patient that you can't learn in your office."

"You must be feeling better," Elizabeth said, interrupting me. She probably feared I would dump all my resentment of the medical establishment on this nice young man. She looked at me lovingly, but spoke more for Mueller's benefit than mine. "You know you would have a fit if there were some treatment you weren't offered because you insisted on home treatment. Look at Nancy Doolittle's crooked arm. That doctor set her bones at home. No X-ray."

"Well, that sort of thing doesn't happen much anymore," Mueller said, "but that's the sort of thing I mean. Only worse. Life threatening. But I have learned the hard way that it can sometimes be life threatening in less obvious ways if the doctor doesn't know much about a patient's life, stuff he's not apt to learn in an office interview."

"When I taught sixth grade in Georgia," Elizabeth interrupted, eager to keep me quiet, "the school board required every teacher to visit in every home every year. I used to wade through red clay mud to visit all the country people. I resented taking the time. But always came home glad that somebody made me do it. I sometimes used to wonder how I had ever presumed to try to teach some of the kids . . . especially the ones who aggravated me the most . . . until I had seen where they lived and met their mother or father or smelled the kitchen."

"But," Dr. Mueller interrupted, "you would have had a hard time lugging a globe around with you . . . or these days, taking a computer in your pocketbook. Even if it were as big as the old doc's satchel."

The codeine was making me feel very good and very sleepy but I managed one uninformed platitude, "For my money we've got too many computers in the schools and too few visits to the homes. Who ever heard of a teacher making a home visit these days . . . not since Coolidge went back to Vermont . . . or John Dewey published . . . what was it? That essay which got credit for revolutionizing public education."

"You sound like a hopeless reactionary," Elizabeth said quickly. "Why don't you go to sleep before Dr. Mueller finds out how difficult you can be."

"I don't know about the schools around here," the young doctor replied. "For all I know they may have thrown out the computers and substituted home visits. I kinda doubt it. But I do believe doctors could up the housecalls a bit, especially with certain medical problems.

"I remember a young mother I treated for ulcers. For a long time she only seemed to get worse. I was thinking about some more radical procedure. Then one day she called me. She was hysterical. One of her children had something stuck in her throat. I rushed out there. By the time I got there the child was OK, but she was really unstrung."

"I should think so," said Elizabeth.

"But it struck me that whenever I had seen her before—always in my office—she was always very much in control. I stayed and visited with her a while. Before I left I had seen her father-in-law take up his rocking chair near the stove, I had heard her husband yell at her for the car keys and wait for her to bring them to him, and I had watched her settle three or four disputes between her children.

"The next time she called for an appointment, I set aside more time. We talked about the choking episode . . . and much else. I listened a lot and prescribed little. It wasn't long until she and I had worked out some different ways for her to manage her pretty tense if not miserable existence. Pretty soon the ulcers were better.

"So, yes, in answer to your question, I do make housecalls. I like to make housecalls. But I don't do it very often. It is important. Sometimes it is very important." He looked right at me with a mischievous hint of a boyish smile. "If I hadn't come right out here when you called . . . who knows? . . . by now you might be headed to surgery."

"Surgery?" I asked a bit sleepily.

"Yes, surgery. To remove the bed pan. What will you have, Reverend professor, local or general anesthetic?" Dr. Mueller brushed the hair from his eyes and smiled expansively. "I don't know which Father Brenkle would choose."

"Father Brenkle?" I asked.

"He's my pastor. You should get acquainted."

I smiled about the bed pan and me and the priest. But inwardly I was tremendously moved by the gentleness in Frank Mueller's manner and the caring in his voice. A stranger in our house with healing in his person.

Elizabeth was not ready to end the visit. "He really gets immobilized when his back goes out," said Elizabeth. "Do you think we should ask you about an orthopedist or some other specialist?"

"I've already talked with an orthopedist, one of the best around," Mueller replied. "He thinks it is safe to leave him here as is for a few days . . . until the pain eases. Keep in touch with me. Then, maybe by next week you can bring him into town so I can see him and decide about X-rays."

"So that was the phone call?" I asked.

"Yes. To Santa Rosa when you get the bill," Mueller said. "But for now, I want to make good use of this housecall."

"We are certainly glad to find you," Elizabeth said, "and relieved. You have no idea. Everything has always seemed good about living up here except health care. I need someone to help me with my hands and feet once in while." She lifted up her left hand which had the most distortion of the joints. "My right one is better. I had it operated on. I have some grasp in it. But my feet! Do you know a good podiatrist nearby? I need to go about once a month or so."

Mueller recognized her gesture and her words but did not really look at her hands.

"I'm sure we can help you find help. That's really how this new breed of family physicians operates. We just want to help you manage your total health. We are not too proud to get you in touch with specialists. That's part of our responsibility."

It was clear that he was concerned and sympathetic, but that was all for now with Elizabeth. He turned toward me, "This is today's patient." And looking directly at me, he said, "What troubles you most about this episode? It's not new for you, is it?"

I felt myself turning to putty with all my sour suspicion melting away. He sounds, I thought, as though he really is interested in me . . . in us . . . in our new situation. And he was taking time.

"No, it's not new. But this time it is unusually severe. I actually couldn't have gotten up off the floor if I had fallen."

"But what worries you about it this time in particular."

"I don't want to get laid up. We have big plans. This is the first time in our lives that our time is pretty much our own."

"Big plans?"

"Yes. And long postponed. We've been on the waiting list for three years for one of the most popular freighter trips that still takes passengers."

"You are going to sea?"

"We are pretty sure now that we will get called about January first. They can't . . . they won't make any promises but the American President Lines' officer has confirmed a date for us sometime between January and March of next year."

"Where will you go?"

"Tell him about it, Elizabeth."

"You're the patient. Go on," Mueller said to me.

"I can't pronounce the names of all those places as well as she can. She's really the literate and informed one here."

"Don't worry," Mueller replied. "She will get her chance . . . sooner or later.

"Well, every trip is different," I explained. "Determined by the cargo. So we really don't know exactly where we will go or how long it will take. So you either have to be retired or be the idle rich to go. But it is freight from West Coast ports to Asia. No guarantees, but the average voyage lasts around 80 days."

"What part of Asia will you visit?"

Elizabeth began calling the ports like an old-fashioned railroad conductor, "'Japan, Korea, Taiwan, Hong Kong, Singapore.' We love Singapore. We've been there once before."

"This trip usually goes much farther," I added. "Sri Lanka and Bangladesh and China."

"Sometimes even to Egypt."

"So you see, doctor, you've got to get me ready."

"I think you'll be more than ready. Have you ever been to a Back school?"

"A what?"

"The Community Hospital in Santa Rosa has a Back school. You go once a week for six weeks and learn about your back and how to use it. But first we need to get you mobile."

Before he left but after we had talked quite a while, he examined me carefully again and satisfied himself that I had not smashed a disc. He helped Elizabeth arrange the bed and improvise some support for my back. Then he was gone. But all the time he never seemed in a hurry. While he was here, he was really here. Present to us.

Within a week Elizabeth was able to get me into the car and into town to keep an appointment at Dr. Mueller's office. Again he spent a lot of time getting acquainted. He and I alone. He asked me about retirement. And what I missed most. And where and when did Elizabeth seem to feel the most uncomfortable with me around so much more of the time.

"Are you a family physician or a psychiatrist?"

"I'm no psychiatrist. But if you need one I'll help you find a good one. Or a surgeon. Or a urologist."

I thought he could just as well have skipped that last example!

"Please don't insist I see an orthopedist. None of them has ever asked me what I was worrying about."

"One orthopedist already knows a lot about you. We agree that for now the Back school is most apt to get you shaped up for Singapore and Bangladesh."

So I went to the Back school. I also bought a money belt to wear in Bangladesh.

But first we had to get ready to drive to Colorado and Arizona in the fall. That would be a good test of my back.

CHAPTER 6

If I Make My Bed in Hell

Not more than two months later, after six sessions in the Back school and other preparations for travel, Elizabeth and I found ourselves stranded in the basement of a Denny's restaurant in Denver, Colorado. Elizabeth's frugality over the years had prompted us to get acquainted with almost every Denny's restaurant and Motel "6" between Connecticut and San Francisco. I think she favored Denny's because there were no surprises. Consistency is a virtue in inexpensive chain restaurants if you like what they are consistent about.

We loved to drive across the country. We made many trips by car since that first one together with the children, the pregnant cat, and the two dogs in July 1960. Elizabeth rescued from the trash a sturdy plain corrugated box with lid intact. It served for years as our travel kit. In this box she maintained all the necessities for comfortable and economic motoring such as sunscreen ointment, a heavy Swiss knife I gave her one Christmas, [the kind that has a good can opener among its multitudinous blades,] a small jar of instant coffee, several cans of grapefruit sections in natural juice, paper napkins and little moist wipes, two matching heavy-duty plastic cups and one of those little electrical gadgets to heat water quickly, shaped like an old-fashioned coat hook such as once lined the hallways of grammar schools at child level where the children were taught to hang their coats and mittens, paired securely with long strings. With this gadget

37

we could have our breakfast coffee without darkening the door even of a Denny's. At night we could have hot soup, out of envelopes, served in the coffee cups.

The trip that took us to Denver was no exception. I went there to participate in a three day continuing education program for the clergy, sponsored by Iliff School of Theology adjacent to the University of Denver. I always welcomed invitations to Denver, the place of my birth. Many times I had given Elizabeth the official tour of my childhood with a long pause before the two story red brick house on York Street across from City Park which my parents had built and where I was born upstairs in my parents' bedroom.

We arrived in Denver in the late afternoon of an autumn day. Driving through the mountains much of the day, we had been filled with the outrageous autumn display of the quaking aspen conspicuous with yellow and gold amidst the green and grey of the lodge pole pine and Colorado blue spruce. The aspen trees, quivering with the last of their energy, silently semaphored all passersby with their massed colorful flags, "We are here, too, in the forests of the Rockies. Take one more look at us before we are left stripped and bare to suffer the winter cold."

Then as we left the high reaches and came down through the lower ranges, speeding indifferently past the miserable little crossroads of junk food stores and taverns and garages, we came at last to that broad opening in the foothill canyon where the prairies, stretching clear to Kansas, come into view.

As children, restless with travel, this was a place for which we watched, competitively, this was a moment of excitement and exclamation. There, where the rocky rough canyon walls were broadened and pushed back into gentle slopes, we could see out, we could see home, the Queen City of the Plains, stretched before us. The lustrous dome of the capitol, where on my fifteenth birthday I got my driver's license without any kind of examination, marked the upper side of downtown. The sharp pointed tower of Daniels and Fishers Dry Goods store, where favored children got haircuts in a tower salon, marked the lower side of downtown. The burnished dome and the graceful tower were visible miles away and had no competition.

Now, on this choice autumn day of 1983, the dome and the tower were suffocated in smog. All we could identify, as the interstate traffic poured out of the mountains, an oil spill on wheels, was a cluster of gross over-reaching narrow blocks of icy grey skyscrapers pushing their swaggering way up through that ubiquitous pall of gaseous fumes which covered the Queen City of the Plains.

We managed to find our way through the urban clatter and clutter to the campus of the seminary. I stopped by the Dean's office to let them know we had arrived and was given the key for the guest apartment by an attendant-secretary who was worrying on the telephone with her baby-sitter about the baby-sitter's boy friend all the time she talked with me. As it was almost dinner time we decided to eat before hunting up the apartment and settling in.

"I know there is a Denny's near here somewhere," Elizabeth said as soon as we had decided to eat first and unpack later.

"This is a big city," I said with poorly disguised annoyance. We had already driven over 400 miles that day. "I don't want to waste time and money driving miles to find a Denny's."

"Yes, I know," said Elizabeth, "but just this once, go on farther out that busy street we came in on. If you don't come across a Denny's within seven minutes, I'll not say another word about finding one."

Her luck held out. Within a few minutes we were on one of those streets full of separated traffic and a separated culture, travellers hunting motels and residents hunting the fastest way home. Lights and signs and claims and counter claims everywhere, plus perilous left turn lanes with drivers, like so many track stars, bending forward at the starting line, impatiently waiting for the signal and held in check only by one disciplined foot on the brake. Then "whoosh," they're off!

We "whooshed," full tilt, into Denny's driveway, afraid to slow down very much for fear some of that separated traffic, of which we had been a part, would push us straight ahead if we slowed. It was still early for dinner and we easily found a parking place for our compact wagon with its California plates and its load announcing we were tourists. The car was fairly well loaded as we were also going to Arizona to visit my sister before we returned home and we had items reprieved from the dump that we were sure she would welcome!

"I hope they have a clean rest room. I certainly can use one," Elizabeth said with a carefully controlled weary edge to her voice.

"Sometimes they're good. Sometimes they're bad. But let's hurry up and find it. I'm ready, too." It was time, I thought, for me to supply energy for both of us.

As we went into Denny's we recognized we had been there before. Although my mother died at my sister's home in Arizona, she was buried in Denver and we had discovered this exception-to the-rule Denny's when we were home at that time. We remembered this one because it had a distinctive arrangement, unique, I believe, in the Denny empire. It had a spiral staircase down into the basement, which people in Denver's dry climate think is a perfectly good place for more than storing potatoes. So, amazingly enough, at the bottom of this fairly long stairway was a pleasant lobby with a few over-stuffed benches against the wall and three telephones separated by scarred plastic partitions. The rest rooms were down there, as well. The carpeting on the stairs was grimy green and rose with the darkest color toward the middle of each step, radiating out to the brightness of the carpet's former glory at either unwalked-upon edge.

"This must have been elegant when it was new," I said with a tired look-around at the fading splendor. "Denny's must have taken over from some fancy eatery that didn't make a go of it."

"All I care at this point," Elizabeth said with the urgency stimulated by a rest stop postponed, "is that the plumbing works."

With that we were down the fancy circular stairs and made our separate ways to freshen up for the Senior Special to be served upstairs with soup or salad—dessert and drink, extra. I returned to the lounge from the men's room and sat down on one of the worn upholstered benches against the wall. I enjoyed watching the people, shadowy figures moving up and down the stairway and in and out of the rest rooms. It brought to mind some theatrical presentations of hell or at least purgatory. All that was lacking were some wisps of hot steam rising up around the edges and rolling out under the doors of the rest rooms. Maybe the water in the drinking fountain is boiling hot, I thought, and all the telephones offer only endless busy signals.

After sitting there a while and watching these candidates for hell descending on the soiled carpeting to disappear into the separate sections of the underworld through doors marked for their sex, it suddenly dawned on me that Elizabeth was unusually slow in joining me. Just then she came out into the lounge and looked around. I did not wait for her to join me on the bench, but got up and went to her for somehow she seemed distressed and was not moving with her usual dispatch.

"I will have to sit down," she whispered when I reached her. She took my arm and we moved back across the room to the bench.

"What's wrong?" I asked after we sat down.

"It must be the altitude," she replied after a moment of sitting still and reaching for her breath. "I noticed it when I got out of the car . . . to stretch on Loveland pass . . . or whatever they call it these days. I was really short of breath . . . it was so strange . . . it surprised me."

"The altitude, of course," I said, vastly relieved. "It's still pretty high here. Over 5,000 feet. The Mile High City. I never thought. Why didn't you say something?"

"It was nothing . . . really."

"It may be nothing to you. But it's something to me. Everything. I do wish you wouldn't be so damned private about how you feel." The irritation in my voice made me regret my words at once.

"I really don't think it's anything to worry about," Elizabeth said, looking at me in a way which said she was sorry and that she appreciated my concern. Her breathing was much easier as she continued. "Don't you remember the last time we went to Tahoe? The Hendersons had a big party. I got pretty short of breath that day. But as soon as we got back down out of the altitude I was fine."

"Yes, I do remember." At that moment I also remembered that the problem at the Hendersons was a very long flight of stairs up to their delightful mountain home. I remembered how Elizabeth tried to disguise the difficulty she was having from all the friends busily chatting on the deck above toward which we were headed. She pretended to stop and look around to admire the view or comment on the wildflowers below the steps. She never looked up toward the people.

We talked about that day for a little bit and then Elizabeth said, "I'm getting hungry. I think I'm all right now. Let's just not hurry."

So we walked back across Denny's basement lounge and started up the spiral stairway with the thick traffic-weary carpeting. Elizabeth took my arm again and held to the banister with the other hand. She moved very deliberately. She paused on the second step. "I just can't do it," she said.

I could feel anxiety moving up into my throat squeezing my speech into senseless small starts and stops. "Rest a minute. Then try again," I said, finding my voice after a moment. "We're in no hurry. We can take all night. If we need to."

We stood there on the second step for a little while with Elizabeth doing her best to look as though we were simply pausing in our ascent to admire the gold-flecked wallpaper, which

was peeling a bit at some of the seams. She couldn't bear drawing attention to herself in public or in private either! She remembered all too well the many times her mother passed out, two
times in particular, once at the Baptist Church back home in Georgia before the whole congregation, and once at Trader Vic's in
Oakland where a lovely friend of ours, Beth McCaffrey, long without a mother herself, had taken her for a special luncheon treat.
Trader Vic's had called for emergency help as though she were
surely dying. Then they called us. When we got there it looked as
though the entire Oakland Fire Department were on hand with
Mrs. Davis passed out in the men's room. The ladies' lounge was
upstairs! Elizabeth knew her mother wasn't dying. At least, she
never had died in any number of such faintings. Elizabeth was
torn between concern for her mother and her own mortification
at all the commotion.

Standing there in Denver two steps up on the stairway out
of Denny's basement, she said she simply would have to go sit
down again, that she couldn't climb those stairs, at least now. I
knew Elizabeth must really be alarmed. That more than doubled
my concern for she was always the cool one in emergencies. We
found a bench near the bottom of the stairs. After she had rested
a few minutes, I said as persuasively and urgently as I could, "I
think we should call a doctor."

"Please, don't," Elizabeth said with as much firmness as her
breathlessness would permit, "I'll be all right . . . It's just those
stairs . . . I don't want to faint . . . halfway up. Then we will have
no choice . . . Denny's will call them . . . sirens and all."

"I'm worried. I think we should do something." I should have
known that was the last thing for me to say.

"There you go," Elizabeth murmured, conserving her breath,
"you always get so upset . . . you always have to do something."

"I don't either," I retorted defensively.

"Oh you do, too," she said. "No wonder I don't tell you when
I don't feel good until I have to." Her breath was stronger as was
her feeling!

What are we doing? I thought. Quarrelling in public. But I
wondered what I should do. Maybe Elizabeth's excessive need
for privacy should not be our first concern. It would be up to me.
I really felt she would soon get acclimated. If not, we were only
going to be in the higher altitude for a few days.

After a long pondering silence I said with a very upbeat tone,
"It does take a while to get used to the altitude. I remember one
Christmas when I was in college. I came home and from sea level

went directly up to Berthoud to ski. It was hopeless. I sat in the lodge all day. When we came down, I was sure glad to get out of the altitude. But it's an easy cure."

"Thank you," Elizabeth said, recognizing my effort to calm down and be reassuring. "This is not a bad place to rest. Let's sit here and talk for half an hour. If I can't make the stairs by then, you can call anyone you want."

"Fair enough," I answered. "What shall we talk about?"

"I don't care. Only I think you will have to do the talking."

CHAPTER 7

Better Is a Handful of Quietness, Than Two Hands Full of Toil

We sat there together in silence for quite a while. I picked up again with my watching the weary people, descending and ascending the stairway of this netherworld, heading for the rest rooms, then emerging refreshed and ready to be fed. Somehow I thought of the Apostles' Creed, that moving poem of faith lost upon those Christians who want their religion spelled out in plain flat language suitable for a pharmicist's directory of pills.

I recently saw a version of the creed prepared for a congregation's use in which some sentimental or literalistic soul had removed the phrase "and He descended into Hell," speaking of the very last place the Apostles thought Jesus must have visited before ascending into heaven. That had always appealed to me. Where else? It's been a tremendous comfort to trust that even in hell no one is beyond the reach of God's loving care, no one is ever beyond possibilities for change, for fulfillment, never beyond the supporting power of God's promise. Even the thought of perpetual damnation is an offense to the God who encounters us in Jesus. So why shouldn't a trip to hell have been a high priority on Jesus' travel plans. I love to repeat that phrase of the creed with special emphasis! It means that I believe when all hope is gone, there is still hope.

Well, here we were. Stuck in a minor little hell. We were, at least, in between worlds for the moment, lost souls of a little league. Our expectations of food were derailed. Certainly we hadn't expected to spend an hour or so in Denny's basement when we came in for their Senior Special. My stomach reminded me of that immediate and temporary disappointment. But what about the long range expectations for the years ahead. I had even begun to ruminate vaguely about that when Elizabeth poked at my sleeve. "Go on," she said.

"Go on?" I asked.

"Go on where?"

"Go on talking."

"Oh, sure. Let's see. Where were we?"

"I had the feeling," Elizabeth replied, "that you were going to come up with something cheery." She looked at me with a wicked smile. "It's all right. I'm ready to be cheered up now, if you think you can."

I had a sudden inspiration.

"Maybe I should try to talk like George Matheson," I said.

"Who?"

"George Matheson, the blind poet and preacher of Scotland who wrote, 'O Love, that wilt not let me go'."

"You don't really think I remember something like that," Elizabeth said with friendly annoyance. "What's he got to do with you and me stuck in Denny's basement?"

"Thanks, my dear. You gave me the precisely right lead-in question. There's a story about Matheson and a cellar. It's about an old lady who . . . "

"Another 'old lady'?" Elizabeth interrupted. "Why not an 'old man' once in a while?"

"Oh, come on," I looked at her and smiled, "give me a chance. Don't spoil the story. Anyway, it was told that there was an old lady in Matheson's Edinburgh congregation who lived in a basement flat. One day she moved to another one on an upper floor. When someone asked her why, she replied, 'Ye canna hear Mr. Matheson preach Sunday after Sunday and keep on living in a cellar.' So you see, if I could talk to you like Matheson preached, you'd be lifted right up out of this windowless hall to a table in Denny's restaurant, a nice clean one by a window, looking out at a magnificent Colorado sunset."

Elizabeth smiled at my effort. "No cellar is a cellar with you."

"Thank you. Nicely said," I replied.

Then she said, "But I'm really not all that interested in old ladies and old preachers. You never have told me what you and John Mitchell planned for him to do while we are away."

Mitchell is a young contractor who had become a good friend. He did a lot of work for us, big jobs and small ones, during the years before we moved up to the country full time. We were forever changing things or adding on. Now, despite all the trips to the dump, we still needed more storage space especially for the improved garden equipment I had bought. So during our absence John was going to tackle that problem.

"Well, all right," I picked up responsibility for the conversation. "We discussed the shed and he is going to start on that. It's going to be a very simple structure with an overhead garage door. He won't get involved in anything elaborate. He's going to haul in a load of heavy gravel and spread it around for a floor."

"That sounds sensible. Is he going to do anything else?"

"If he has time, he will put in a stronger fence around the vegetable garden."

"Did he think he could fence out the gophers?" Elizabeth asked.

"Not really. But he is going to put it 18 inches into the ground. That may discourage the old and tired ones."

"Did you talk with him about adding some more storage space in the kitchen?" Elizabeth asked.

"I didn't say much. I thought he should talk directly with you. But I did ask him if he would have time in the spring—after we're home from the freighter trip—if we decided to do any major work, like improving the front entrance. He didn't make any commitment. He just said something about evolution."

"Evolution?"

"He says our house is as bad as the Winchester Mystery House. You know, the one in San Jose where the woman thought as long as she was adding on to her house, she wouldn't die."

"That's really awful when you think of it," Elizabeth said thoughtfully. "Morbid. Is that what you are doing with the constant remodelling? Fending off death? I sometimes think you regard death as the great enemy."

"I'm afraid you think right," I replied quietly.

"Think how horrible it would be if nothing ever died," Elizabeth said with dismay.

"Sounds good to me."

"Think about it," Elizabeth continued. "How would you like Mrs. Winchester's house rambling all over the city of San Jose and filling up the county and then the state. It'd look great covering up Yosemite. Think of the whole earth filled up with senile plants and people, non-productive."

"That's all well and good for death in general. What I worry about is my death in particular."

"Why do you think you should be an exception?" Elizabeth asked reasonably.

"There is some comfort in that," I said, "in its universality. But that doesn't help much. The fear. The reluctance. I wish I could have your composure about it. But there is so much more that I want to do and be before I die."

It felt somehow appropriate but eerie to be talking like this stuck down in the bowels of Denny's basement with its dim light and random procession of shadowy figures hunting the drinking fountain or going to the bathroom with an occasional one trying to get an urgent-sounding call through on the pay phone, sending a message up and out and back to the living, as it were. "But you could send me a money order at Herb's" . . . "Ruthie's sick . . . we'll never make it tonight" . . . "Don't hang up, damn you . . . Christ-a-mighty . . . Shit" . . .

If Jesus were around anywhere He was incognito. But, then, how else does He come?

"You are never content as you are," Elizabeth continued. "You always want to have company. But as soon as they come, you wish they'd go home."

"Oh, that's not true!" I protested. But I shuddered a little inwardly. It was too near to something that was true. I was always looking forward. The future always more interesting than the present so that when the company came or the porch was remodelled or the trip was started, I'd had it. What was next? I didn't argue with her. I didn't deny it. She was right and I knew it. But I didn't know she knew it, too. It was a sad secret.

Perhaps that is the source of my annoyance at Holy Communion when the service is cut short and the eschatalogical affirmation is skipped as of no significance, namely, "We do show forth the Lord's death until He comes." No liturgist ever cuts out "This we do in remembrance of Him." Strange, isn't it, to make memory more important than hope. Life is really suspended somewhere between the two. I wondered if Elizabeth was more into memory and I was more into hope. Well, memory is demonstrable and hope is not. And Elizabeth's college degree was a B.S., not a B.A., in science not in the arts! But if that were true, why was it I and not she who has the trouble with death?

"That is just restless you, I guess," Elizabeth said kindly but quickly. "So why should I expect you to be content with the house as it is. If we weren't taking off on that freighter trip, you'd have John Mitchell out there every day building something."

I felt a bit defensive but then I remembered another house, a house that rambled everywhere because of life, not death. Now I'd finish off old Mrs. Winchester! "Elizabeth," I said excitedly, turning upon her like one who has just thought of the perfect way out of a corner. "Mrs. Winchester doesn't have a corner on adding on rooms. If we had come in on old US 40 today, we would have gone by another house, if it's still there, that is always growing. Or, at least, it did for years.

"When we were little kids and Mother and Dad owned the sawmill at Fraser, we went back and forth between Fraser and Denver all the time, some of the same road we were on today. We had an old Cadillac touring car. It wasn't old then. It was quite elegant with two spare tires on the rear covered with some shiny black material like plastic. Must've been oilcloth. The trip took most of the day. Sometimes the folks would plan it so they went over Berthoud Pass at night because they could see the headlights of cars coming and wait at a turnout and not have to back up to pass.

"We were all interested in a house we went by many times in Clear Creek Canyon above Idaho Springs which seemed to grow a new room every summer. It got so it sprawled out all over the countryside. I wonder if it is still there. My father solemnly explained that the owners had a new baby every spring. That's why they added on the rooms."

"I like Mrs. Winchester better," Elizabeth replied with a hint of her rebellious side in her voice.

"Careful," I warned laughing, "careful. There was another Elizabeth, you know, who had a baby past her time."

Elizabeth smiled, but went on about Mrs. Winchester. "She's not so sunny, more realistic, not so 'God's in his heaven and all's just great in the world.'"

"It seems to me," I countered, "the guy preparing for the babies was as realistic as Mrs. Winchester fighting off death."

"If he were realistic," Elizabeth answered, "he could have stopped the babies. I'm being contrary, I know. But I honestly think you'd be a lot happier if you could discover why you always have to be in a stint to change things. So restless. Every moment should be savored for itself, let tomorrow take care of itself."

"Here you are," I replied, "so short of breath you can't climb the stairs out of this cellar and still savoring the present moment?"

"We might never have had this conversation if we hadn't been delayed here," she countered. "In some ways the hour we've spent stuck down here has been one of the nicest hours of the day. And so far as the house is concerned, I would think you would get tired of being unsettled . . . perpetual confusion. It feels more like Mrs. Winchester's fear of death to me than hope for more babies . . . It's too frantic to be good. What are you running away from?"

Elizabeth was addressing me very soberly, very tenderly. She continued, "You are never quiet. You always have to have some project. Even in retirement. Especially in retirement. Now when we have a chance . . . "

She stopped short and looked away.

"A chance?" I prodded. "A chance for what?"

"A chance," she began again, slowly, reflectively, "a chance for us. A chance to enjoy one another . . . and this whole beautiful world around us. We don't really live in Denny's sunless basement."

She stopped and looked at the people moving around the lounge. She touched my arm. Pressed it with her tightly closed hand, bound by arthritis like the bound foot of some aristocratic Chinese woman we worried about as children in the mission study class.

"For me," she went on, "it's just enough for us to be together, have time to read and watch the changes on Mt. St. Helena. We've never had time. Time together. Not since Pemaquid. And not really then. Life is depth of years as well as length! Why are you always rushing off somewhere? Do you find the grass greener here now that we are on the other side of the Rockies?"

I was quieted by Elizabeth's view. Her words did not feel critical. They were loving. Maybe Jesus had descended for a moment into Denny's basement. Sometimes it felt as though she had a private access to me that even I didn't possess. As I grew quiet, her pragmatic side spoke up, "Besides, more house is always more to care for. I want less not more. I wish we could let things be for a while."

This was an old argument between us. I felt that we would never change *anything,* except plants and animals, if I didn't push. At the moment I was too worried about Elizabeth to get very fired up over her charge about my fears. But the Winchester bit had hit a sore point. I answered passively but I suspect she sensed I was on the edge of being mildly angry. That was about as angry as I ever allowed myself to be with her, which was a problem in our marriage. But I was defensive, thinking it was well that one of us had some energy and interest in the house.

I replied with just a bit of attack in my voice, "You never seem to get tired adding another few feet to the garden for some special English peas or . . . whatever."

We had come to the usual impasse. Elizabeth looked at me and, with a very loving hint of intimate amusement, put a period on the argument when she replied, "If it's babies you want to justify next year's addition to the house, you're looking at the wrong woman."

That was evident as we sat there in Denny's basement. It certainly wasn't morning sickness which was keeping us there in an evening holding pattern of sorts. But Elizabeth was right. I was restless about life . . . incomplete. She seemed able to find completeness in the present. I always needed something to look forward to.

Retirement was no exception. But in retirement what could you look forward to? Death! No wonder the distracted life of the segregated adult communities surrounded with their golf courses and handcraft shops and social rooms is so attractive. I could be tempted by all that busyness. Not Elizabeth. Sometimes I felt she lived in a different world. She needed only the hummingbirds to feed and white crowned sparrows to watch or a valley oak to rescue or a tiny violet to nurture . . . or a grandchild to hold. With that she was at one with herself and her creation, and her Creator, too, I suspect, although she seldom spoke of that relationship.

There was the whole world in her hand, complete in that moment, and death when it came would be part only of that moment, not this. And it would come like a friend, aware of some need to be supplied. She would welcome it as a friend. I was sure of that. But how could she feel that way? 'Natural as a leaf slowly falling toward the compost,' she once said. I knew she really felt that way. It was all she expected and enough. But I did not understand. I had high expectations, but not of death. My "friend" was world travel, lots of company, a new deck to enhance the patio, maybe piano lessons. It felt as though she had another "friend." I did not know. But now, she was weary from the talking and we both grew quiet although I continued to mull it over in my mind.

CHAPTER 8

Make to Yourselves Friends

Elizabeth was right, I thought to myself, as we continued this unexpected vigil in Denny's nether land. As retirement had grown nearer, I had talked more and more about continuing and accelerating our perpetual "developing" of the property. Maybe it was fear of death, as Elizabeth suggested, but I had certainly enjoyed the remodelling we had done over the years before my retirement.

As an unexpected benefit, Elizabeth would readily agree, we discovered that this was a quick and pleasant way to get better acquainted in the community. We had been part-time residents for years. We only knew our nearest neighbors, the Hafeys and the LaBarees, who were friendly and kept an eye on the house in our absence. But once we started remodelling the house and adding on to it, we met all kinds of other wonderful and interesting people.

For example, there was Arnold Enderlin, the electrician, who has upside down bi-focals so he can see what he is doing over his head. He is a generous man, once on the school board and a long time elder in his church. When you need him in an emergency (he babied our pump for years), you drive around town until you see his beat-up purple van. Years ago, when we first started some serious remodelling of the house, Arnold told us about a young man, named Mitchell, home from Vietnam, who was building up a contracting business.

51

I called him and he agreed to come out and talk with us about what we wanted done. This was long before we added on the master bedroom and bath. We had decided such major work might never get done, certainly not until we were through paying for our children's education, but in the meantime we could give the old bathroom a face lift to tide us over until the new one could be built.

At the appointed time I heard Mitchell's truck in the driveway and went out to meet him. "I'm Browne Barr," I said. "And spare me any jokes about my name. I've heard them all."

"You think *you* have problems," he answered, as he unfolded himself out of a small Toyota pick-up and extended his hand, "My name is *John Mitchell.*" During that summer Watergate filled every news' broadcast. That week, I believe, Martha Mitchell was giving her husband, John Mitchell, Nixon's attorney general, a hard time. To be named John Mitchell was a laughing matter as the White House John Mitchell squirmed to make right out of wrong.

I remembered how this John Mitchell, the contractor, seemed to fill the house as he came in to meet Elizabeth and talk with us about what we wanted him to do. He filled it not so much with his well-proportioned and disciplined body, but with a radiance, a glow of countenance. He smiled easily and laughed deeply. Although he was tall and powerfully built, he moved so gracefully that you wanted to see him run or catch a football or swing a beautiful ballerina safely through the air.

"Arnold Enderlin told us about you," I said. "Do you want to fool around with fixing up an old bathroom?"

"What do you have in mind?"

So the three of us crowded into the bathroom. Elizabeth and I sat on the edge of the immense old stained tub, which our cattle-raising neighbors still have out in their pasture as a water trough for their magnificent Black Angus. Perched there unsteadily on the tub, we tried to explain to Mitchell what we had in mind. We soon discovered that he understood us readily. But then, without seeming to put our ideas down, he gently carried us on further with his own creative genius. We had thought a new sink with a fresh counter made of some sturdy stain-proof material like formica would do nicely. Of course, there would have to be a new tub with a built in shower. No question about that.

"Well, that would be fine and I can do it," he replied quietly. Then he added, in regard to our proposal for the washbowl and counter, "But don't you think it would be a shame to put a plastic counter in this bathroom? Those walls are good clear redwood."

So it was. When the job was done our remodelled bathroom did not look like it came from a Sears' catalog. The counter was sand-colored ceramic tile bordered by a few tiles with hand stenciled splashes of bright blue and dark red which Mitchell found along Telegraph Avenue in Berkeley. The pulls on the drawers were old-fashioned crystal knobs he found in his collection of such stuff. And the light fixture was a row of clear bulbs over a massive mirror which made the small dark room seem large and light.

As the years passed and Mitchell did other small jobs for us in our endless "developing" of the property, we learned how he had toyed with a career in architecture and then, later, had actually applied for law school. Then he lost his deferment. He made no bones about not wanting to go to Vietnam but his life moved inexorably relentlessly in that direction—Marine Corps, OCS, Naval Flight School, Pensacola, attack helicopters, Camp Pendleton, February '68 and the Tet offensive, a hit in the copter transmission, crash, a big piece of windshield and a chunk of rotor in his thigh, severed artery, rescue team flew in, "I couldn't hold on to the sky hook so the crew chief jumped on to hold me." The Vietnamese started shooting again, now at this huddled target swinging in the sky. "The pilot dragged us into the plane, got blood and morphine started and flew to a field hospital, they tried to save the leg, moved me to Saigon, then to Japan. I got maggots, gangrene. I went up three times for amputation and each time it was postponed . . . two years later I got discharged with both legs and permanent disability . . . . "

I cannot believe that the Vietnam fiasco was necessary for the making of the strong-caring person John Mitchell became. But I am sure that his response to all that agony of spirit and body made the crucial difference. He spoke to me only once about that chapter in his life but it was not his only struggle. He came back into old expectations, spent two years at USC and got a MBA degree. His wife, Karen, his college sweetheart whom he credits with getting him through college, worked at UCLA through these years.

Then all set to be commuters and ride the button-down collar business track, Karen and John Mitchell balked, sold everything they owned for $6,000, packed a small trunk to be stored with their parents, and lived in a VW bus for two years as they wandered across Asia. When they came home this time, they had the courage to do what they wanted to do and settled in the wine country and worked with their hands, as well as their heads, and won recognition, Karen for her catering and baking, and John for his carpentry and design. They had not allowed expectations, theirs or others, to strangle their possibilities: A good rule for youth, but it takes guts . . . and resistance to pressure!

One spring day John was working away at a porch we had decided to add at the front of the house. I heard him come into the kitchen to consult with Elizabeth.

"Oh you can't do that!" she exclaimed with horror.

"I'm afraid I will have to, Elizabeth, if that is where you want the porch."

"Then forget the porch," Elizabeth replied.

I was in the next room. Such a strong response. My curiosity was stirred. I went to the kitchen as though to get a drink of water. Elizabeth was up to her ears in tomatoes. Water was boiling on the stove. She was in the middle of dropping the tomatoes in the water and then quickly pulling them out in the large slotted spoon and squeezing the hot skins off. Even then her hands were so twisted by arthritis that an observer could hardly keep from staring. Not at her hands, but at the inventive and ingenious ways she managed to handle those hot tomatoes. She finished up the batch she was working with and set them aside for freezing later. They could wait while she dealt with John and now with me. John had been waiting patiently for her to come to a stopping place.

The steam rising from the stove and sink had not cooled Elizabeth about the porch. She looked at both of us as she spoke, "John wants to cut down that little laurel tree to make room for the porch."

"I don't *want* to cut it down," John interrupted with a cautious smile. "You make me sound like a criminal."

"Well then, please don't!"

"That's OK with me," John said amenably, "but do you want the porch two feet narrower?"

Where is King Solomon? I thought. But I held a cautious silence.

"Let's go look at it?" Elizabeth said.

So the three of us trooped out to the front where John had been working. He had been lining out dimensions of the porch so he could get the foundation poured the next day.

"I see what you mean," said Elizabeth. "If you save the tree, the porch will be pretty small. Also won't you have trouble with the door if you cut the porch back right there?"

"Oh, yes," said Mitchell. "I really can't do that. It would be tacky and you'd never like it."

"But you can't cut down that tree." It was Elizabeth again.

"There's a magnolia right around the corner," I said. "No shortage of trees."

Elizabeth looked at me darkly. "You can't be serious."

I didn't dare admit I was. So I tried another tack. I turned to John, "Can't you work around it?"

"Around it?" replied Mitchell. "What do you want me to do? Put a notch in the porch? It would look like someone had crashed into it with a back hoe."

"Wonderful!" said Elizabeth, smiling broadly right into Mitchell's worried face. "A notch? Why not? That's a great idea. John, you're a genius!"

Mitchell groaned. "That's going to push up your costs. I'm really trying to hold to the budget."

"And how much do you think the life of that little tree is worth?" Elizabeth responded as though it were her offspring. "You could never move it."

So we ended up with a notch in our front porch. Except for complicating the roof line and the gutter, it really worked out quite pleasantly. On one side of the notch is a stand for a fern and the screen door; on the other there is a corner for a comfortable chair and a reading light. A visitor once commented that she had never seen such a charming porch. "It certainly pays," she said, "to have an architect."

When John returned to work the next day, he brought a fresh loaf of bread from Karen's kitchen. "Karen sends her congratulations to Elizabeth in the laurel tree battle," he said.

All of this seemed very far away as Elizabeth and I sat there in Denny's basement. We had stopped talking as Elizabeth seemed to be tired by the effort. I enjoyed ruminating on the happy prospect of our retirement. We had not been plunked down to grow old among strangers like many older people who have to move when they retire. Indeed, it was John and Karen Mitchell who gave us a welcoming party the day after we moved in to stay. I presume there might well have been a beautiful welcoming party if we had moved into a plush secure adult community. But the hosts would not have been a delightful couple on the threshold of interesting careers. They would have been people pretty much like us, more or less; not so these new friends, the gifted contractor, Mitchell, nor the gifted physician, Mueller.

I wished we were down out of the high altitude, out Denny's basement, and safety home amidst the vineyards and friends in the wine country.

CHAPTER 9

Would God It Were Morning

I don't know when I had stopped daydreaming and started "resting my eyes" there beside Elizabeth on a bench in Denny's basement. It had been a long tiring day. I came to with the awareness that Elizabeth stirred at my side. "Mr. Matheson," she whispered, "wake up."

"Oh, you remember my story." My voice was only half awake.

"Of course, I do. I've heard it three times," she said in a gentle teasing voice. "It's a sweet story."

"Sweet? Damn! I hate that word."

With that Elizabeth got up. "Sweet or not. Have it as you like, Mr. Matheson. But start preaching because I'm ready to be elevated."

I got up and joined her. We moved toward the stairs. Elizabeth took it slowly, stopped a couple of times to rest, but was much recovered and made it to the top. We rested again as we paused in front of the sign which reads, "Please wait here to be seated."

Soon the hostess appeared. I asked, "Do you have a table next to a window, please?"

She invited us to follow her and showed us to a table beside a large window. We sat down. Immediately Elizabeth looked out the window. "But oh," she said. "It's almost dark. I guess we missed the sunset."

I did not reply. I had shuddered inwardly when we reached the top of the stairs and noticed there was no Colorado sunset pouring through that restaurant's windows, only a bland twilight from a sun retiring without glory behind the frontal range of the Rockies. We were out of hell but we had not ascended into heaven.

It was not like it had been when I was a child. No wild reckless blazing sunset from one end of the range to the other and reaching out and up, like endless golden streets, to the high center of the sky. The smog, the curse of our disobedience, took the glory from the twilight and shortened the lovely ending of the day into the darkness of an early night. Had we rested in the cellar longer than we thought? Too long? Oh where was the preacher of Edinburgh!

After dinner Elizabeth felt much better and we went on back to the apartment, but she let me do the unpacking. I wished I were packing to leave. What had happened to me in this day of return? I wondered. Was it only the pain of learning afresh that you can't go home again? Or was it my anxiety to get Elizabeth out of this beloved high country of my childhood which had now turned hostile to us? Maybe it was a bit of both, a strong taste of life's evening. It was bitter. I would have no more of it.

Three long days later when I finished my stint at Iliff and we were packing up to head to Arizona, Elizabeth carefully folded a sweater and laid it on top of other clothes in a very full suitcase. Then she sat down on the edge of the bed beside the open suitcase. "I never knew the altitude also affected your energy," she said. "I have never felt so weak in all my life as I have since we've been here. I will certainly be glad to get to Arizona. Scottsdale isn't high, is it?"

"No," I replied. "I suspect Scottsdale isn't much higher than Calistoga. A few hundred feet, maybe."

"Good. Then maybe I'll get back some energy. I'd like to help Irene a bit."

My sister, Irene, had sold her house and was preparing to move into a retirement community. She had indicated she would like some help sorting over some of our mother's things which she had stored for years. We hoped she would be ready for some help with the packing chores. When we arrived we quickly saw that Irene would welcome any help we could give. The next morning we all went to work.

Elizabeth took on the task of packing the good dishes. She had stacks of newspapers on the counter and wrapped the fragile pieces carefully after she assembled them in small groups from the shelves above her. Irene showed her the ones she did not want to trust to the movers to pack. Elizabeth was very careful and deliberate about such work. I knew she would be especially careful because these were Irene's treasures. She was also pleased, as she told me later, because Irene did not seem to regard her hands as inadequate. So I did not think much of it when I noticed her working very slowly and pausing in the wrapping several times as though she were figuring what would next fit best into the packing box. After a while she plowed through the confusion into the living room to retrieve the kitchen stool. She took it to where she was working and hoisted herself up on it and continued the wrapping. She is so short that I had never before seen her sit down at any kind of reaching or wrapping job.

Before it dawned on me that it was not her hands which were bothering her, I overheard her say to Irene, "I'm sure not much good to you today. I just don't know where my energy has gone lately."

"That's a miserable job you've taken on," Irene replied. "Stop for a while and join me for a cup of coffee."

"I don't know what is wrong with me," Elizabeth continued. Irene is one of the few persons in the world in whom she ever confided. "Ever since we were in Denver, I've just been no good. No pep. No energy. I should have stayed home."

"You've been working at that longer than you think," Irene replied. "Sit there and take it easy for a while. I'm going to bring you a box of costume jewelry I plan to give to the thrift shop. Look it over, please, and tell me if there is anything there that you think I shouldn't give away."

I admired my sister's sensitivity about not pushing Elizabeth more about how she felt. They both always seemed just to accept each other as they were. That afternoon while Elizabeth was resting in the bedroom with the door closed, I poured out my rising concern to Irene. Not only is she very slow to give advice, but even more, I learned early in life that I could tell her anything and it would go no further.

One time when Irene was probably over 50 years old and most of the persons concerned were dead, my other sister, Faith, and I were speculating about what ailed a distant cousin we liked very much and with whom we played when we were children. After Faith and I had tossed the question back and forth for a long time and proposed many explanations, Irene finally entered the conversation and said in a matter-of-fact way, "He had epilepsy." When we were children many decent people were ignorant and uncomfortable and sometimes cruel in their view of epilepsy.

"Why do you say that?" Faith asked.

"Because he had an epileptic seizure one day when we were playing in their backyard."

"He did?" I was incredulous. "You never told me that."

"No."

"Did you tell mother?" Faith pressed.

"No."

"Why not?" I asked.

"Aunt Clarita asked me not to say anything about it."

"Did you ever tell anyone?" I pressed.

"Not until today," she said quietly. "I don't see how it could hurt now."

"How did you know it was epilepsy?" Faith asked.

"I didn't. It was a long time before I figured out what was wrong with him."

Irene had contained that bit of sad but newsworthy family information for "well over forty" years because she had said she would. No wonder Elizabeth trusted her. But it was sometimes maddening when you knew she knew something very, very interesting which she wasn't about to tell!

Later in the day I helped Irene sort over the accumulation in her linen closet. I was urging her to radical action in reducing her holdings. "You will never use that!" or "How long has it been since you've needed fancy finger towels!" It is so easy to get rid of other people's stuff. While we were bantering back and forth about scores of washcloths and half used bottles of white shoe cleaner, Irene took occasion to speak to me privately about Elizabeth which was unusual. She scarcely ever interfered in my affairs and was very stingy about advice even when it was solicited. Also, she wasn't about to violate any confidence but she knew that I had been in the same room when she and Elizabeth had the conversation about energy levels.

"When you get home," she said very simply, "don't you think it would be a good idea for you to encourage Elizabeth to see that young doctor you've been raving about?"

"Of course. She must," I replied. "The problem is to get *Elizabeth* to think it would be a good idea."

"I don't see that it could do any harm," she replied as she turned back to sorting some linens.

"Then why don't you suggest it yourself." I was hunting reinforcement. "She thinks I rush to the doctor when all I need is a couple of aspirin. You know she would listen to you."

"She's not asked me for advice. She's only wanted me to listen."

Although Elizabeth was ordinarily slow to take the lead about almost anything, I did not have to encourage her to make an appointment with Dr. Mueller. The very next morning after we got home, she called his office and got an appointment for the following Monday afternoon. That was a very long weekend for me. Occasionally I would come upon her sitting at the table by the window but not really looking at anything. Once I said, "Penny for your thoughts." As soon as I said it I felt I had intruded. She only smiled and pulled herself together as though to say, enough of that. It's time to be up and doing.

Monday noon, as we finished lunch, she said, "I can do the shopping when I get through at the doctor's."

"Don't forget the cat litter," I replied, "or we will soon be in a crisis."

"What else do we need? Let me get my list." With that Elizabeth left the table and went to the kitchen counter and came back with a narrow piece of blue paper she had rescued from somewhere. She finished up a list—milk, meat for tonight, cold cereal, litter, 2 lemons, Ajax, lettuce, and a few other items all grouped on this narrow piece of blue scrap paper according to where they would be found in the store, working from right to left, or east to west, whichever way you view the universe.

After she left I went out to the shed John Mitchell had finished in our absence. I rigged up some shelves for garden supplies and then wound up two garden hoses which I had dumped in the shed. I wanted to wind them up in neat green circles to store for the winter. One of them was pleasantly compliant, yielding to my tugging like a child neurotically determined to please the authority figure no matter the cost. But the other one, made of stronger stuff, defied my authority and kept springing back into the shape it had determined for itself like a gigantic cowlick which pops up even when you grease it down. I thought it strange how that recalcitrant one annoyed me but won my respect. I drove some enormous spikes into the wooden walls and hung up the two circles of garden hose, one still refusing to be round or flat. They would stay there until spring.

Then I went to work on the woodpile. I enjoy splitting the kindling. For me it is a "one glove job." I need a heavy glove to protect my left hand as it steadies the piece I am splitting and protects me from splinters. But if I wear its mate on my right hand, I cannot grip the handle of the hatchet firmly and it tends to slip. So the working gloves around our place are like some couples, always separating. When you come upon one, it is not at all certain you will come upon the other nearby. It was a lovely sunny afternoon and it felt good to be home on our acre with Mt. St. Helena standing guard.

I had not yet started to keep one ear alert for the sound of Elizabeth's return when I heard the gravel being crunched by the slowing wheels of a car in the driveway. I put down the axe and went around the garage toward the front of the house with the glove still on my left hand. It was Elizabeth. She stopped in front of the house where we usually left the car when we had groceries to unload. She did not get out at once. She sat there as though she did not want to get out and face me. Why was I intruding into her isolation? She seemed to be saying. Don't push me, don't rush me, don't press. I got here too fast. I'm not ready. Not ready. Not ready to come home. Not ready to get out.

I went around to the driver's side whereupon she began to stir to open the door. She backed away from the door handle so she could get at it better with her less crippled right hand, but she managed to release it only partially and the latch caught on the safety catch. She tried to pull it shut again to engage the latch. Without success. She fussed again with the handle.

"Oh this door," she said with intense frustration. "I can't get it. Damn!" She settled back into the seat and gave up altogether on the door. Then I saw a tear collecting itself and taking shape in the edges of her eye.

"What's wrong?" I said as I came alongside the car and opened the door. But she didn't move. She just sat there and looked straight ahead as though she had not heard me or seen me.

"Lizzie. Lizzie, what is wrong?"

She turned then slowly to me like a fluctuating needle in a gauge, finding its focus, its registration. At last she found her voice.

"We can't go," she whispered.

"We can't go? Can't go where?" I asked.

"To Singapore."

"Singapore? What is this about Singapore?"

"Not Singapore . . . or Bangladesh . . . or China. Never."

"Never?"

The tears had eased out from her eyes and rested tentatively on her cheeks. "Never . . . never. He was very kind with me, but, clear, so clear . . . My breath, my energy . . . It will only get worse. I've known it. I really have. But . . . I kept hoping . . . months, maybe a year or two. . . ."

"Oh Lizzie, no . . . no . . . you mean . . .," but I could not bring myself to say it. "What is it? What did he call it? Did he give it a name?" How we think we can drive something away, control it, master it, if we know its name. I could feel my knees begin to shake, my hands growing cold, as though all the warm blood of my body had drained down through hollow funnel legs straight into the earth. I was glad I was beside the car.

"Heart . . . congestive heart disease," she said slowly, so softly I could scarcely hear. Then she slid out from behind the wheel and eased her feet down to the distant ground. Elizabeth did not ever "get out" of the front seat of a car or truck, she dismounted like a diminutive equestrienne leaving a riding horse.

She landed easily in my proffered arms. As I looked over her and closed the car door behind her, I noticed there were no groceries on the passenger seat where she always put them. There was nothing there except the limp half of the seat belt. It looked as lonely and as useless as the single glove which remained on my left hand.

As we walked away from the car a narrow piece of blue scrap paper floated lazily silently from somewhere on Elizabeth's person and came to rest in the grass alongside the driveway. It was a list of groceries never purchased, expectations dropped silently along the roadway.

CHAPTER 10

My Soul Is Cast Down Within Me

I followed Elizabeth into the house. I tried to find words to fold in lovingly around her but there was no speech in my mouth. The tide of woe set loose by the words spoken in the driveway swelled soundlessly, uninvited, into the house and picked up every private personal thing waiting in its path, plans for dinner that night and freighter reservations with the American President Lines, prize roses to be planted, whale watching at Pt. Reyes, picnics in the winter sun—picked it all up without asking and crudely threw it like so much cast off sodden litter on the now desolated beach of our expectations.

Elizabeth was moving on ahead of me down the short hallway from the kitchen to our bedroom. Her steady, unhesitating step suggested she did not want to deal with me just then. Larger matters pressed their priority and their privacy. I felt a gentle curtain drop between us. I could not chase her. I must not pursue her. But I needed to ask, to learn more, to hear that I had not heard. I stopped in the kitchen and stood at the sink. I turned the water on. I turned the water off.

Elizabeth walked into our bedroom. I heard her close the door behind her and turn back, as it were, into the dressing room which was a buffer, filling the space between the kitchen storage wall and our bedroom. It was very quiet in the house. I heard the birds chattering at the feeder outside the kitchen window. Oddly,

I wondered if there were hummingbirds at the feeder by the other kitchen window. I turned and saw one, poised upon its quivering wings beside the bright red cylinder, drinking repeatedly deeply.

Elizabeth was in the dressing room and I at the kitchen sink, unwillingly estranged by the rough intrusion of our mortality. It sequestered us in that fragile aloneness in which we are born and in which we die. We were under one roof, our roof, but separated by a wall, a storage wall, a wall of trappings and necessities and belongings, a wall of our living. On one side two racks of clothes, two dressers, a mirror, a comb and brush . . . and a woman, and a bell tolling; on the other three cupboards of dishes, a skillet, a dust pan and broom and a narrow little shelf for sweet basil and salt, thyme and dill and coarse ground black pepper . . . and a man, and the echo of a bell tolling. How long we were alone, I do not know. It was all time. It was no time. It was harbinger. It was hell.

In that silence I must have heard her coming, I do not remember, for I turned from the sink and the window and the birds. I turned, and there she was. We were drawn only to the other without sensing anything, any movement, any sound, nothing except being whole again in full embrace.

At last Elizabeth moved her head back to look up into my face, "O my darling," she said softly, clearly, "that this should happen. To you. It's not fair."

Now she was holding me. And all I was holding tightly of myself was released. It emerged not in cries, shrill and sharp, but in vacuous gasps, almost silent, reaching deeper and deeper for breath. Strength and weakness, life and death, came together in a consoling harmony. And there in her arms, my arms grew strong again. My arms and my hands and my legs connected with their intensity once more.

At last Elizabeth carefully released me and said, "I think I had better sit down." Strength and weakness. Life and death.

I poured a glass of ice water from the refrigerator jug and placed it before her. She sat at the table where we eat. It is half in the kitchen and half in the living room. We eat there and we live there. Then I poured myself a small jelly glass full of jug wine and sat down at my usual place. Also at the table.

"Do you know what I've just remembered?" Elizabeth asked with a warm little laugh in her question.

"No."

"The groceries. I forgot to go shopping."

"I know," I said, not meaning to upstage her. "What is more I know where your grocery list is. It is out in the driveway. You must have dropped it when you got out of the car. I just left it there. It didn't seem important."

"It's important, all right," Elizabeth answered. "If you want any dinner tonight. We don't have meat or milk."

"Let's both go shopping," I suggested.

So it was.

* * * * * * * *

Christmas came and went pretty much as usual. Winter and the rains came. The days were quiet for us with this largely hidden secret for constant company. We made a strained effort to push out of our daily life the enormity of Elizabeth's prognosis, but it was brought painfully into our days when Elizabeth couldn't quite finish getting dinner on the table or took forever to get dressed. It pushed in especially vigorously on the two afternoons we went to Santa Rosa to visit the specialists with whom Dr. Mueller had made appointments for her. First there was the specialist in pulmonary diseases. Then on another day we had our first encounter with the cardiologist.

Frank Mueller had managed to temper my bias about physicians, especially primary or family physicians like himself. His informal style and reflective manner made you feel that you were a whole person winning his concentrated caring concern. You were not a "case" or "the three o'clock" extracted from the waiting room. My critical view of the medical profession never had held up very well in encounters with actual individual physicians. It was badly shaken by Roger Hedin, our physician friend in San Anselmo, and now almost shattered by Dr. Mueller who confessed to me one day that sometimes he thought there was more priest in him than medic.

But the specialists! Ah, now, I thought, as we approached the pulmonary fellow, we will be back on the impersonal assembly line. We may even have an encounter in person with Jim Nelson's caricature. Nelson, a friend, a theologian, an expert in medical ethics, once wrote a devastating description of doctors as the high priests of a culture whose god is science.

I don't remember precisely how he expressed it, but I have often thought about it when waiting my turn in a doctor's office. You wait patiently, without complaint. The doctor's time is sacred, yours is disposable. Finally a frizzy headed young woman appears like an acolyte, calls out your name, your first name, your baptised name if you are a Christian, calls it out as an assistant to St. Peter may call it out on Judgment Day. You respond quickly, eagerly, apprehensively. She escorts you into a small sparsely furnished white cell, assures you the doctor will be with you presently, and leaves you to twiddle your thumbs, look at a blood red chart of the circulatory system, or pray.

Finally the high priest appears. He is dressed in white, a symbol of purity against your impurity, with a stethoscope around his neck which he fingers like a rosary. After you have made your confession and he has looked you over for other possible signs of disease, the new high priest writes out a prescription in eucharistic Latin which you grasp and protect like a holy token. In the days which follow you obey the high priest's instructions—"religiously" we say.

So we went to face these two specialists. Unfortunate creatures! They didn't know what dark suspicions they faced in the silent husband who accompanied this patient of Frank Mueller's who was so short of breath. When the "specialist" himself, rather than a fuzzy headed acolyte, came out into the waiting room to greet the new patient, the defusing of the arrogant silent husband began. It was continued when the "specialist" made it comfortable for the patient to choose to be accompanied or not to be accompanied by her husband. Elizabeth invited me to come with them into the inner sanctum.

This specialist in pulmonary diseases, Dr. Solomon, was living up to his name. He was taking time to establish a relationship and a base for confidence before he so much as looked at a chart or felt a pulse. Somehow we learned that he had moved to Santa Rosa from the Bay area for the sake of his growing family. We also learned that he had a Yale connection. Then you should have heard me. I pulled out all the stops on our Yale connection.

"Yale?" I said. "Why I was at Yale in the fifties."

"Yale College?" he asked.

"No. I was on the faculty . . . Divinity School."

I am embarrassed recalling this bit of conversation. But what did it mean? What was I saying? Such inordinate self-promotion or advertisement! Here was I, the powerless, reaching shamelessly to regain some power, quite willing to humiliate myself with braggadocio to gain special treatment for Elizabeth, my love.

I think maybe I was saying, "Look, fellow, we're somebody, too. Please. Please. This quiet lady beside me. She's important. She's loved. Don't treat us casually. Treat us special. Care about us. We are worried sick . . . please . . . help us. Give us your best."

Certainly when you feel you are on an assembly line in a doctor's office, pushed along from room to room, technician to technician, with a turnstile at the exit marked "Pay Here," when that is your experience, you may feel well examined but you seldom feel well cared for.

We had already been spoiled by Frank Mueller who often seemed to learn more about our health through casual conversation than lab reports. But this specialist to whom he had directed us, this pulmonary physician, utterly disarmed me and my readiness to complain about doctors when, ending his examination, he stuck a thermometer into Elizabeth's mouth and said, "When I don't know what to say, I take temperatures." With that slowingdown exercise completed, he then dealt with us in unhurried fashion. Afterwards we realized he had told us how hopeless Elizabeth's situation was. But he told us with a sense of genuine sadness that he could not honestly give us much grounds for hope. We felt that he was sorry, too, just as a fellow human being. We also felt he would have been as kind and humane with someone to whom Yale was a lock to be picked, not a connection to be exploited!

"I think you might like to consider using oxygen a bit," he finally said to Elizabeth.

"Do you think that's really necessary?" Elizabeth asked with a soft rising inflection which expressed disdain and alarm. "I really get along pretty well with my breathing except in the high altitudes."

I found myself turning cold again. Oxygen? It felt like a proposal to prepare for final rites. And if she had to be hooked up to an oxygen tank, she would never see anyone or go anywhere. She would be an instant recluse.

"It's not just for the breathing itself," the doctor explained, "but to give a lift to your heart and your energy. The oxygen can prolong your life by two years."

That sounded like good news to me. Not so for Elizabeth. She looked at him directly and finally said very distinctly, evenly, "Are you trying tactfully to tell me I have only two years to live?" There was a note of challenge, almost belligerency, in her question which alarmed me. It set her apart for the moment from us two healthy men as though she were alone and could not depend on anyone else to protect her and defend her interests.

"That is not what I said," he replied gently. "No one can predict how long anyone will live."

Elizabeth made no further inquiry about the oxygen. There was a heavy silence among the three of us.

"We won't worry about the oxygen today," Dr. Solomon said at last. "You will want to talk to Dr. Mueller about it. I will report our conversation to him."

A few days later we visited the cardiologist. Again Dr. Mueller had encouraged me to accompany Elizabeth. Certainly we were in this together. Dr. Price, the cardiologist, was also skilled and humane. He struck a good note with us when, after asking Elizabeth if Dr. Mueller had tried a particular procedure and being told he had, he found an appropriate way to express his high regard for him professionally. "You've got one of the most skilled primary care physicians in this whole area," Price said. "He never misses a bet."

He took Elizabeth into a nearby examining room. After he had finished extensive tests, he invited me to join them. It became immediately apparent by his hesitation that he couldn't find an easy way to tell us that Dr. Mueller's diagnosis was clearly right. But he did not need to search for the appropriate words. Bad news does not really need to be spoken. It is in the shift of the teller's shoulder as he struggles to find momentum for the first merciful phrase of explanation. It was evident to us that this doctor, this human being before us, found himself with a difficult task. That he found it so was a strange source of comfort to me. We are so bound together in the human mystery that genuine concern, even from a stranger, when we are in pain is encouraging, supportive.

We left the cardiologist's office without an appointment for a return visit. I stopped at the bookkeeper's window and signed some forms and left a check. Elizabeth and I walked slowly toward the elevator. She stopped to admire an immense rubber plant flourishing in the three storied atrium of this new professional building. She told me its Latin name and expressed surprise that it was doing so well in the environment provided. By the time we finally reached the parking lot and found our car, Elizabeth was very weary. I knew it for sure when she declined one of our favorite indulgences, a Baskin-Robbins ice cream cone. So we drove directly home. After all this exposure of body and soul we needed the protection of the private place we loved.

"How do you feel about today?" I asked her, as we drove down Franz Valley Road nearing home in the late afternoon sun. The vineyards, with their pruned and dormant vines, looked like regiments of wooden soldiers, their drill halted ankle deep in fields of yellow mustard.

"I am glad we moved to the country," she replied, looking around appreciatively at the valley lush after a winter rain.

"Well, so am I," I said, "but what about today?"

"How do I feel?" she repeated the question without taking her eyes from the dormant grapevines and the greening hillsides. "How should I feel?" she asked at last. "The other shoe has been dropped."

It was a closing reply to an opening question. I am glad she did not leave it open by asking how I felt. I would have had to stall, also. For how does one tell how one feels when hope has been left with the doctor's cashier?

So we settled down "to make do," as an old Vermont friend often said, "to make do" with our changed and limited circumstances. Our expectations for our retirement all shot to hell. I think we both were comforted by the suggestion that oxygen, when Elizabeth was ready, might well add two years to her life expectancy. We held on to those words like a reprieve proclamation. So, at least, we had that much time.

Maybe we could retrieve some of our expectations, a modest trip, perhaps, instead of the ambitious one to Bangladesh! But even so . . . such a short ride. We had yet to discover that it can be very ordinary expectations that hide us from extraordinary possibilities. That is a hard lesson to learn, that lesson about expectations and possibilities. Through the next few months I was deaf to every teacher it sent.

CHAPTER 11

Bring Quickly the Best Robe

We were not very far along on that shortened ride, a few weeks at most, when I noticed that Elizabeth had an appointment with Dr. Mueller on her birthday. I had not given very much thought to my responsibility in our changed circumstances. I was glad I was available to take over any household chore when I saw Elizabeth was tiring. I tried to be alert but mostly, I guess, I thought it was my responsibility to provide distractions and keep us busy and occupied. I was the morale officer on a cruise ship to eternity! Operating uncritically on that supposition, I had a wonderful inspiration. I would give Elizabeth a surprise party!

If I got busy, I could manage it even if her birthday were only a few days away. I knew that the doctor's appointment was in the morning and she would probably need to rest most of the afternoon. I figured that would give me time to pull together the meal itself if I could get some of it catered.

However, before I could order any food I had to get the guests corralled. Whenever Elizabeth was out of earshot, I would get on the telephone. We have an incredibly crowded roster of loving friends within driving distance of our country acre. Finally, I managed to find six of them who could manage to be free on such short notice for that weekday night. My nephew, Bob, and his wife, Joan, were among them, but even they were not aware of the extent of Elizabeth's problem. She was never comfortable talking about her health to friends, and people who knew her best would hesitate a long time before asking. Her arthritis had become increasingly obvious over the years, but the sorry condition of her heart and lungs was not known except to our children and our sisters.

After I got this modest guest list established, I went to talk the party over with Karen Mitchell who had a highly praised catering business. I think she suspected I shouldn't afford her services. Probably she had overheard me many times complaining to her husband, the contractor, about costs. "Cost plus?" I had chided him one time when I received a bill, "It looks mostly 'plus' to me!" Of course, that is only paranoic speculation on my part. It *was* very short notice. And she was genuinely sorry, but she couldn't take it on. She suggested I talk to the chef at one of the Calistoga restaurants which serves excellent if pretentious cuisine. Cuisine, mind you, not food!

I found this young man in his kitchen during the afternoon lull. I suspect he was a recent graduate of one of the culinary schools now much in vogue. He was very helpful and I especially liked his suggestion of fresh salmon baked in a pastry crust. He said he could do that for fourteen dollars. I thought that was surprisingly reasonable. The salmon alone would surely cost almost that much. All I could have done at that point in my culinary career, fancier than hot dogs, would have been steaks or a standing rib roast, either one of which would have cost that much or more. Perhaps I looked puzzled because he suggested that he would also include a sauce for the salmon, a large bowl of lettuce greens and some fresh strawberries for dessert. That really amazed me.

"Why I can hardly afford to eat at home," I said.

"Well, the price is better than in the restaurant," he explained in a strangely defensive manner as though I thought he should charge more, "because once you pick up the food, our responsibility is over. For that price there is no delivery, no dishes, no serving, no clean up, just the food."

"No problem," I said, pleased with the deal I had struck.

"But do serve it hot," he urged with a creator's fervor. "Don't pick it up too long ahead of time."

"Of course," I assured him. "My nephew will pick it up right at six. Is it all right if I pay you now and have that taken care of?"

"Either today or tomorrow is all right with me. Let's see. There will be eight of you, didn't you say?"

He turned over an opened envelope lying on the counter and pulled a pencil from his top apron pocket and did some figuring. I thought I could figure the tax on $14 in my head.

"That will be $112," he said. "Plus tax. I think that's right. Eight times fourteen. I will put in some fresh cookies, too. They will be nice with the strawberries. They are magnificent berries. The first ones from the Imperial Valley."

I reeled inwardly as though he had pulled a gun on me. But at once I realized how stupid I had been. Of course, $14 each! This surprise party was surprising even me! It was too late to back down. At least, it was too late for me. I felt as foolish as I do when the waiter stands around waiting for me to test a newly uncorked bottle of wine. Never in the world would I let him know how inexperienced I am. Oh well, I thought, what's a hundred dollars more or less. This may be the last birthday party we can have for Elizabeth.

The next day was the day of the party. Elizabeth went to the doctor in the morning and it gave me a chance to fix some shrimp and cheese and carrot sticks for hors d'oeuvres. We had retired not only with four davenports but with two refrigerators. One we kept in the garage for storing fruit and vegetables and jugs of wine. So I had hidden stuff out there and had time to prepare it and hide it again before Elizabeth returned from the doctor.

When she returned, I couldn't believe what I saw. She came walking in with a black box the size of an old fashioned camera hanging down her front like some grotesquely overgrown onyx pendant suspended on a chain heavy enough to have been purloined from an ancient gravity feed toilet. And about as graceful!

"And what is that lovely little ornament?"

"Oh, it's a gadget I have to wear for 24 hours."

"For 24 hours?"

"It monitors my heart."

"Can't you take it off while you eat?"

"Oh, no. It's all set. I suppose what your heart does when you eat is as important as what it does when you go to bed." She was smiling seductively, trying to joke about this latest development. She seemed to guess that I was distressed, but I presume she thought I was distressed about her.

"I don't mind wearing it. We don't have any plans to go anywhere, do we?"

"Oh, no. We'll be right here."

All I could think of was an earlier conversation we had that day in which I had said if I were fighting a battle with my health I would want everyone to know about it. I'd want all the support I could muster from whatever quarter. Elizabeth couldn't understand my feeling. She said she wanted no such invasion of her privacy, and that her friends respected that, and she loved them for it.

After lunch Elizabeth went to the bedroom for her afternoon nap. All afternoon I rushed around getting the table set and being glad that she slept so soundly and wondering if there were any way I could defuse the explosion that was building up like steam in a stuck pressure cooker. The guests were invited for six. Around five I heard water running in the bathroom and knew she must be stirring. I put on an apron and went into the bedroom just as she returned.

"Are you getting supper tonight?" she asked, seeing the apron.

"Yes," I said. "I'm experimenting. I thought I'd take over and surprise you with a new dish. This is for your birthday. So do me the great favor of staying in the bedroom until I call you. Then I'll have it all ready. Here's the morning paper." I put it down on the bed. "I'll turn on the radio so you can tell me all the news." I turned it on slightly louder than usual.

By six all the guests had arrived except Bob and Joan who were getting the food. The bedroom, separated from the kitchen by the dressing room, is at the back of the house and I was sure Elizabeth had not heard them. I had toyed with the idea of going into the bedroom on the pretense of examining the black box more closely so she would take it off long enough for me to push her into the living room. That was no good. There was nothing to do now but to plow ahead!

So I called for her to come out and groaned inwardly and wanted to run and hide as she opened the door. She was something to behold. The heart monitor machine was hard to wear with ordinary clothes she explained later. So she had put on a roomy housecoat she had loved for years. It always felt so good that she continued to wear it even though she couldn't get a large brown coffee stain out of the left sleeve. She was ready for a comfortable evening at home.

"Surprise!" It was a feeble and embarrassed greeting from the uneasy guests who recognized at once that she was not even ready to receive the friendly septic tank repair man much less dinner guests. After a very bad moment, Elizabeth laughed. "Surprise, indeed!" Her welcoming smile for them was strangely blended with a menacing look in my direction.

The evening went well for everyone, even for me. Elizabeth saw to that. She was unflappable in her sincere graciousness. In any social situation, Elizabeth focussed so honestly on the person before her that no one would ever guess what physical pain or emotional turmoil was tucked away for later attention. I believe that she was actually so centered outside herself when she felt responsibility for other people, that her own pain, her social discomfort, retreated. So this surprise party, building up to a potential social catastrophe, was . . . well, it was no triumph, but it was not a disaster.

When the guests left and the last red tail-light had grown dim down our driveway, then vanished over our bridge, she sat down in the chair by the fire and lit a cigarette. "You really are a dear," she said. "This is a night I'll never forget."

"For more reasons than one," I added chuckling. "When you came home with that gizmo around your neck, I thought the jig was up."

"Its lucky for you," Elizabeth said with a lovingly scolding tone, "that I never had the slightest suspicion or I would have locked myself in the bathroom for the duration."

"You were magnificent when you made that grand entrance," I said. "You faltered only a second. Then you laughed and your face lit up and everyone breathed easily again . . . including me!"

"Well, it really was quite a shock," she said. "But thank you anyway, it was a lovely party. How did you do it?"

"It took some doing, I must admit," I replied. "It's lucky we kept that second refrigerator out in the garage. I stored everything there. Neither you nor the mice could find it."

"You didn't hide a baked salmon in the garage. Where did all that good stuff come from? Karen's?"

"It was good, wasn't it?" I replied basking in her honest praise. "Karen was busy and couldn't do it, but she suggested a guy in town."

"I bet it cost a fortune," Elizabeth said, not critically but appreciatively.

"Not as much as if I'd taken you to the Highlands for dinner and overnight. You will laugh when I tell you about my arithmetic." I moved toward the kitchen with my fingers deep into some water glasses.

As I searched for some clear space to put them down, Elizabeth said, "Oh, come sit down. I'll get my wind in a few minutes and help you clean up, but first we need to talk."

"You talk while I clean up," I answered. "I can hear you all right. What about your visit to Dr. Mueller? What's he going to learn from that heart monitor?"

Elizabeth did not respond at once. I thought she was waiting for me to come nearer where I could hear better. After several moments she said in a gentle tone of voice, "Well, I guess that's what I want to talk about . . . that, and the party."

Although I was turned away from her, headed with more dirty dishes to the kitchen, I recognized in the evenness of her voice that she was troubled. I had better forget the kitchen mess and go sit down. Could it be that there was some new bleak news carried into our lives in the black box hanging in the folds of her worn housecoat, the breakfast-stained housecoat, in which she had partied all evening?

"Just a minute," I said. "Let me stick the coffee cream and the butter in the refrigerator." I did so. I returned and sat down in the other chair near the fireplace. "Is this monitor bad news?"

"No. Not really. It's not quite like that," Elizabeth said. "I'm not worried about the monitor. It is just more evaluation. I don't know how to say this . . . but please try to understand. And I really did enjoy the party tonight after I recovered from shock. And I love you for it. And I know it was lots of work. But, please . . . please. How can I say this?" She stood up in front of the fire and threw what was left of her cigarette far back into it. There would be no remnant stub in the ashes. Finally she sat back down and looked at me imploringly. "Let's just not have any more parties. What do you say? Especially surprise parties."

I felt I had been hit right in the center of my belly.

"No more parties?" I said quizzically. "What else are we to do for fun? I don't mind the work. I rather like it. If you'll plan the menu and tell me what to do." Somehow I faintly suspected I was not addressing the question. What was bugging her? I didn't blame her for being embarrassed tonight. But we didn't need to get into a mess like that again. Did she really mean that she didn't want to see people?

"Please don't argue with me, at least not tonight," Elizabeth said with all the life drained from her voice. "Let's just not have another party. That's all I'm asking. At least for a while." She said nothing more. She just looked away from me into the fire as she stroked Abby, the cat, who had sought her lap as she always did when Elizabeth provided one.

I was really upset and not willing to let it rest for now. She wasn't the only one who was tired. "I can't see why you don't want to entertain if I do the work."

I was stunned when Elizabeth turned to me. Her eyes were deepening. When she is growing angry her eyes don't flash or blaze or anything so obvious. They smoulder, grow smokey dark. "Can't you understand! Can't you try to understand anything?"

I knew she was angry and I hated it, but I was getting angry myself. "What is there to understand?" I fired back. "That heart monitor? That you've got problems?"

"It's not that," she shot back. "You understand that all right."

"What in heaven's name is it then?"

"I'm not sure. Maybe . . . maybe it's that you want me to be a guest in my own home."

"That's not true," I bristled.

"Oh yes, it is," she came right back, "I didn't do a thing tonight. I just sat. I didn't even boil a potato . . . much less make a pie. It was your party . . . or some caterer's!"

"But you were the perfect hostess," I retorted. "You made the party. You put everyone at ease."

"Sure," she replied, gathering steam. "Reclining like some Asian queen in this awful housecoat while you got all the strokes."

"Oh," I said. Some light was finally reaching me. "But this was your birthday. It was a surprise."

"I know that," Elizabeth answered soberly. "And you were wonderful to do it. And I really appreciate it. But I'm thinking about the next party and the next. We can't keep on having birthday parties for Elizabeth."

"I'm sorry." And I really was. I thought I was beginning to understand what she was saying. But I had some feelings, too. I was thinking, so that's all the thanks I get. I hated myself for being angry. Anger was never allowed in our household when I was a child. I still confuse it with hatred. I was hurt and I was angry— but hatred? No. I hated our circumstances but even in this heated exchange I was hurting for Elizabeth as well as for myself. It was hard for me to sort out all these feelings. I felt torn inside. I was also very tired.

Then it hit me. I felt a deep hopeless emptiness. Something was gone. Was this the first of many losses to come? For I realized I was arguing with a sick Elizabeth, not the well Elizabeth with whom I had many healthy open hot arguments through the years with all that delicious steam to soak in tenderly when they were over. And on some beautiful occasions, more than steam.

But I couldn't level with a sick Elizabeth. I couldn't argue any more with her about how we couldn't just drop out and become a couple of hermits. It was like hitting someone who is already bruised and defenseless. I was sickened inwardly as it dawned on me that, from my point of view, we were not quarrelling as equals. I felt I had to give her a handicap like playing an adult game with a child. I wasn't being honest with her because I wanted to protect her from the truth.

"It was all right tonight," Elizabeth said, "because it was my birthday. And it was a surprise. And I enjoyed it. But what excuse will we use next time?"

"Oh, Lizzie, my love, I'm sorry. I'm sorry. More than sorry. Much more," I said, going over to her chair and touching her awkwardly as I stood beside her. And I really was sorry. More. I was grieving with her. But for myself, too.

That feeling was much more searing, far heavier and hurting than my first anger over the heavy questions which clogged my secret inner self, questions of life and daily meaning: What is there left in life for us now? What are we meant to do? Just sit here on this acre and rot! These questions faded before the first touch of grief. Oh Elizabeth, my little Liz! Had I already lost part of her? Dear God! But I didn't say anything more.

There was lots of work waiting in the kitchen.

Later that night as we settled down together in the bed, Elizabeth said, "I think we need to talk some more."

I turned over on my side as I replied, "I'm bushed. We can talk tomorrow if you still want to." The next day we were heartily cheerful. We did not talk any more about parties. Not for many months.

CHAPTER 12

My Harp Is Tuned for a Dirge

Shortly after Dr. Mueller had told us there was no way we could safely go on a freighter trip and be many days at sea, I received an invitation to speak at the Community Church of Honolulu. This church was brought into being fifty years ago by Chinese students at the university who wanted an English-speaking congregation. It has flourished over the years and a special anniversary committee invited me to come help them observe their 50th anniversary. The congregation remains strongly Chinese. Many of those students, who pressed for an English-speaking congregation, have become influential persons in the civic and commercial life of Hawaii. They are gracious and generous people and in their invitation warmly included Elizabeth. We would be their guests for a week.

Dr. Mueller encouraged us to go. However, he made it clear that Elizabeth would have to use oxygen during the flight. He prepared the proper request for us to give to the airlines. When we arrived at the San Francisco airport we found United Airlines all prepared for a passenger needing oxygen in flight. We were invited to board early. At our place a small tank was anchored to the floor beneath our feet. When we were settled the stewardess explained its use. She told us to relax, that there was nothing to it, and that she would keep an eye on us in case we had any questions. Few of the other passengers were aware of the special equipment Elizabeth was using. We had a comfortable trip.

78

But the return trip on a different airline was a different matter! At the airport we were told that the equipment was on board and not to worry. When we boarded the plane we had to hold up the line of boarding passengers in order to tell the attendant that Elizabeth was the one who needed oxygen.

"Oh just sit anywhere you like," said the attendant as she took our boarding passes. She looked past us to the next one in line.

"But my wife will be using oxygen for this flight."

"I don't know anything about that," the attendant replied.

"We made arrangements for it when we made our reservation," I replied.

"We must let these other passengers on. Just sit anywhere," the attendant said, reaching around us to offer the next passenger a cheery greeting.

By this time Elizabeth was not only concerned but embarrassed. "I knew I shouldn't have come," she said.

"Don't worry. It'll be OK," I assured her.

We found two seats halfway into the plane. The seating arrangement offered three places on each side of the center aisle. We claimed a window seat and a middle one. The plane was filling up rapidly with people and colorful shopping bags and fragrant leis. As more and more of the passengers got settled, the aisle began to be less crowded and I began to be very anxious. From my window seat it was difficult to catch the attention of a passing stewardess. Finally, one stopped to find out what I wanted. She was not the one we had spoken to when we boarded.

"My wife must have oxygen for this flight," I said with obvious urgency.

"You should have made arrangements," the stewardess replied.

"But we did," Elizabeth interjected.

Without reply the stewardess left. After a few minutes she returned with a slip of paper in her hand. "Yes," she said, "oxygen was ordered for this flight. We'll see what we can do about it."

There was no one now, except attendants, moving in the aisle. I saw the dispatcher preparing to close the door. I pushed the call button. No response. It was awkward and difficult to get out from the window seat but I got up and started to crawl over Elizabeth and the person in the aisle seat. Just as I was suspended halfway over this stranger with one leg and one foot out in the aisle and the other somewhere in the vicinity of Elizabeth's lap, the second stewardess came hurrying down the aisle with a large greenish oxygen tank. I pulled back and sank down in my seat, but not before I noticed nearby passengers taking an interest in this "emergency."

The stewardess asked the aisle passenger to get up. Then she put one knee in the empty seat and handed the tank over Elizabeth to me. She then handed Elizabeth the tubing and showed us how the valves worked. Then she backed away and indicated to the aisle passenger who was still standing that she should take her seat. She said to me in a commanding voice heard by people all around us, "Hang on to that tank. It's like a bomb, you know, if you drop it." The woman in the aisle seat gave a nervous little laugh. Every eye around us was riveted on that tank . . . and on Elizabeth.

A couple of hours later, after everything quieted down and we had managed somehow to poke around the tank at a miserable meal, and the passenger in the aisle seat had fallen asleep, we confided to each other that, painful as it might be, we would rather suffer private indignities than move the tank to go to the bathroom. Elizabeth said very firmly, "If I ever get off this plane, I'll never get on another."

As the plane carried us nearer San Franciso and home I thought to myself how my life was being narrowed down. Elizabeth didn't want to risk any more parties, but I love them. One of the most beautiful and difficult things Elizabeth ever did for me was to give me a 60th birthday party. As I thought about it, I realized that the surprise birthday party I had given Elizabeth, I really had given more for myself. No more parties, she had said.

Now she was giving up travel. Unlike the parties, I knew that was something she, too, would miss. We enjoyed short trips with a picnic lunch; and we worked together for months anticipating long trips like the one on the freighter. I loved being on the go. How could I settle down just to take care of her and a house in the country where we never saw anyone unless we walked out to the highway or drove to town. How soon would I be climbing the walls!

I was shocked by my resentment. How can one love so much and yet hold so much resentment? I found myself thinking of a scene I have spent thirty years trying to get into perspective, trying to be freed of the haunting guilt it provokes. When my first wife died, it was our children, then four and six years old, who concerned me the most. I was unprepared to help them deal with that loss and did everything wrong in an ill-advised effort to protect them. It is no wonder, I now realize in retrospect, that the children's behavior soon reflected the unattended wound deep in their inner beings.

Sue, the four-year-old, developed a fecal obsession which utterly baffled me and left me feeling helpless and wholly inadequate. She also showed an unrelieved sadness, a deep melancholy which shadowed her life for years. Within a few months, Chris then six, began having screaming nightmares. Many a night his shrill cry stabbed me in my sleep. I went to him and picked him up, carried him out into the upstairs hall where there was a dim light. I sat at the top of the stairs in a wretched drafty parsonage which I hated, wrapped him in a knitted blanket his mother had made for him, and held him in my arms and whispered sounds of comfort and wiped his tired wet face until his breathing quieted and sleep began again. These episodes of fecal play and midnight terror went on intermittently for many months, the melancholia for years. If only I had helped them cry!

Each solitary episode stirred my grief and pushed me deeper into my loneliness. I was alarmed one night to find myself bitterly scolding my wife, "How could you do this to me? How could you go off and leave me to manage alone . . . ?" Then I was oppressed with guilt and my misery deepened.

So it was now, by the mysterious process of hidden association, that I remembered an Easter sermon I once preached. A member of the congregation made fun of it. He dubbed it "The Geriatic Special." I don't know how that sermon came about except that I was challenged by an enigmatic text in John's gospel. It occurs one full chapter after John's account of the resurrection so I presume I thought it was fair game as an Easter text.

There in the plane I could not have quoted that text accurately but I remembered the burden of it. I have since tracked it down. "When you were young you fastened your belt about you and walked where you chose; but when you are old you will stretch out your arms, and a stranger will bind you fast, and carry you where you have no wish to go." (John 21:18)

Had I been carried again where I had no wish to go? Was I back at the top of lonely stairs in a darkened house? Was I angry with the one I had come to love so deeply, the one who had helped me so patiently and wisely in my own becoming, angry with her for being ill?

It was profoundly complicated for me because I realized that I was most angry when I thought that maybe, just maybe, "the stranger" who had bound me fast and carried me where I had "no wish to go" was Elizabeth's refusal to stop smoking years ago when I did. As the plane settled down into the Bay area, a geographic area which Elizabeth and I would never again leave together, I was oppressed once more with guilt.

CHAPTER 13

Be Angry But Do Not Sin

In the autumn of 1935, before Elizabeth and I had even heard of each other, we each left home to attend excellent progressive colleges. As a bold symbol of our maturity and independence, we both began smoking cigarettes. It was a mild form of rebellious behavior common among our generation, especially among those reared in restrictive families, where the use of alcohol was regarded as a sure and slippery road to hell and where tobacco ran a close second to alcohol as an agent of the devil. Less was said about the evils of tobacco in Elizabeth's home than in mine. Her father smoked a pipe in his study!

When we were married I was eager to be free of my addiction to cigarettes. I was even more eager for Elizabeth to be free of her addiction because I had a Victorian sexist bias which made me cross with myself for falling in love with a woman who smoked! Perhaps it was wishful thinking, but it was my understanding that Elizabeth and I had agreed that we would stop smoking after we were married. She had no such recollection! Several times I proposed that we "take the pledge" together. She always resisted.

Finally, after we had been married five years, I managed to stop. Elizabeth was helpful in the painful process. One night I had genuine withdrawal symptoms. I perspired so heavily we actually had to get up and put dry sheets on the bed. Elizabeth cooperated in every way. But she would not even try to stop. Her smoking continued to be an unhappy issue between us.

82

"But you don't even try," I protested to her one day when I was urging her to quit. We had taken our patio chairs out under the immense valley oak which gives afternoon shade over the camellias and dogwood and persimmon in our front yard. We each had brought a book to read and Elizabeth also clutched a package of cigarettes and a lighter.

"I don't want to stop," she said.

"Even when you know how I feel?" It felt like betrayal to me.

"But you don't listen to how I feel," she replied evenly as she picked a long white low-tar, filtered-tip cigarette out of its cellophane protected package.

"How do you feel? Tell me. I'll listen. Really I will."

She was quiet for a long moment. Then, very deliberately lighting the cigarette she had just extracted from the package, she inhaled deeply. She held it in her twisted and almost useless hand. She held it out away from her body. She studied it as though for the first time. There flashed in my mind the occasion when I brought her from the garden a single red rose, uncannily perfect in its blooming. She looked at it so intently and for so long that I thought, why I have never looked at anything like that, what have I missed?

Now, not taking her eyes from the cigarette, she said quietly, "I feel that cigarette is my best friend. To think of never having another is more than I can bear." Then she fully opened her eyes toward me. They glistened with her secret torment. Even the leaves of the great valley oak seemed to be stilled by the long silence between us. Finally she whispered hoarsely, "I *can't* stop."

Those words came from her with a strange urgency which frightened me. I somehow knew that this "friend" she feared losing was not my competitor although I was jealous of the hold it had on her. That "friend" was in a different category.

In the months that followed I began to understand that it was "friend" to the little girl who proudly brought the skirt she had hemmed to show to her mother and was told that it was all puckered. It was "friend" to the short, tubby, dark-haired adolescent who longed to be tall and slim and blonde. It was "friend" to the college senior who excelled in anatomy and organic chemistry but was advised not to apply for medical school. Her parents told her she was not strong enough. It was "friend" to the gracious hostess who had to give herself a pep-talk before every social occasion. Every addict has a "friend" in his or her worst enemy.

When she learned how ill she was and when Dr. Mueller made clear to her how important it was for her to stop smoking, she cut way back. I noticed then that her addiction seemed to be to a behavior pattern as much as to an addictive substance. She was often satisfied to go through the ritual, the handling, the lighting, the mechanics, and take scarcely a puff of tobacco. She increasingly became one of those many smokers who simply light a cigarette and put it down. When Dr. Mueller inquired later about her battle with cigarettes, she made a truthful but ambiguous reply. The result of that conversation, in which I pointedly did not participate, was that Dr. Mueller thought she had stopped smoking and Elizabeth thought he had said that two or three puffs a day probably wouldn't hurt very much.

In handling the guilt she felt about her smoking, it was comforting to her that the experts did not agree on which was more responsible for the condition of her heart and lungs, arthritis or cigarettes. She settled for the arthritis! As the months passed I tried not to show my unhappiness about her smoking, particularly after I recognized what a profound addiction it was. But sometimes I could not hold my peace. I was angry about the disappointment we were suffering, and when I ached to do all the things we had planned for our last years, her smoking didn't help. It was no "friend" to me. It was my deadly enemy. When I recognized how much hurt and anger I harbored because of Elizabeth's smoking, I was shocked . . . and then hounded by guilt. After all, it was she who was dying, not I.

As the weeks moved along Elizabeth discovered increased difficulty in doing the work she had always done. She began to run out of energy half through folding the newly washed clothes or before she could finish getting dinner on the table. One noon I was standing around trying to be helpful when she pushed past me a bit more brusquely than was her usual fashion.

"If you will kindly get out of the way," she said, "I will . . . "

"You will what?"

"I will appreciate it."

"Thanks."

"Oh, I'm sorry . . . but it's just about all I can do to get things on the table without you hovering over me." She was angry and upset.

Without a word I retreated to the living room like a scolded puppy. In a few minutes she announced that lunch was ready and we began the meal with an atmosphere as cool as the tossed salad.

"I'm sorry I spoke so sharply," Elizabeth said about three forkfuls into the pasta Alfredo.

"That's OK. I know it must be hard for you."

"That's no reason to make it hard on you, too."

"Do you think they can be separated?" I asked. My voice was shamefully petulant, but I was hurt. I was thinking that it was about time she recognized how hard she was to help. "You remind me of Marty."

"Marty?" she questioned. She well knew who Marty was and what it was we often said about her.

"You know what we say about Marty. How she's all 'give' and no 'take.' How she's never learned the grace of receiving?"

"No 'grace of receiving'!" Elizabeth exclaimed. "That's an awful thing for you to say. So you think I lack grace in all this. Thanks! That's up to you to judge. But receiving! I'm the judge of that! That's all I do. That's what my life has become! I can't do anything but receive anymore . . . with or without grace!" Then with eyes shining with the hint of tears restrained, she looked right at me. "Can't you understand? I do nothing but receive from you all the time. I've given out on my half of our partnership. Now you water the garden and feed the cats and make the bed half the time. And now the cooking, too, which I dearly love . . . All I do is take, take, take—all from you, great big strong healthy you!"

"Hey! Hold on," I protested with gathering stress. I had not intended to stir up a storm. I avoid them at all costs.

"*You* hold on," she said with vigor.

"But that's not fair." I said. "It's not fair . . . to you . . . *or* to me."

"Fair or not. It's true. You listen for once. I do nothing anymore but receive. And mostly from you!"

"*You* listen," I cut in. "That really isn't true. You do far more than . . . " I wanted to reassure her but the truth was not very reassuring.

"How would you like it," she rolled on with energy released from long restraint, "if you couldn't do what you've always loved to do? I can't even transplant a pansy or make up a pot of chicken stock. And when I try, there you are, hanging around, ready to take over the minute I sit down to get my breath! How would you like it if every time you started something you couldn't finish right then, I was hanging around, over your computer or behind your chair, to take over the minute you stopped to rest!"

I was boiling inside. I got up from the table, fooled with something at the sink and tried to collect myself. Here I am waiting on her hand and foot and she complains about my being around. "What the hell am I to do?" I exploded with long repressed anger. "Shall I just evaporate . . . and then reappear like magic when you give out . . . and all of sudden I become useful again . . . needed . . . and come running when you clap your hands!"

"Oh, don't do that," she said with fire in her voice. "I can't stand it when you act like that."

"Act like what?"

"You know very well what I mean. Like a spoiled child."

"So now I'm acting like a spoiled child. It's all right for you to be upset, but when I'm upset, its childish . . . And *you* can't stand it!"

"No," she shot back. "It demeans you. It destroys everything good between us. Just stop it!"

"And everytime you light a cigarette? I suppose that doesn't destroy anything? Demean anyone?"

Elizabeth turned white. Instantly silenced. She looked at me with such pain that her eyes were locked with it, rigid, fixed with disbelief. It must be the way a woman looks at a man she loves who has just struck her across her face. She sat there and looked at me, unblinking, cold. I froze standing at the counter. I wanted to climb in under it and pull the pots and pans over my head. It was the worst moment of our life together, a moment which stretched to our beginning and to our ending. In that unredeemable silence Elizabeth quietly gathered herself up and left the table.

She went to the drawer where she kept her cigarettes, half-hidden under a miscellaneous collection of potholders. She took out an open pack and poked around in the drawer for a particular lighter she could manage. She couldn't find it and came up with a folder of matches we had brought home from a San Francisco restaurant. I thought, she will never be able to strike that kind of a match. It was the kind I always had to strike for her, the kind which often bends when you try to use it if you don't pinch it tightly. Then she headed out to the little deck off our dressing room, a private place where she often went to smoke and think.

O dear God, what have I done? I thought. I've said it. The forbidden word, the direct attack, the low blow. I had vowed I would never say another word about her smoking unless she brought it up. Now I had used it to attack her when I was angry.

CHAPTER 14

Do Not Let the Sun
Go Down on Your Anger

When she was gone, I found my legs again and started out the opposite way toward the door which leads to the garden and the woodpile. I hesitated at the door and turned back and went to the table and started to pick up the oven-proof bowl of pasta Alfredo. It was still very hot. Damn! I went into the kitchen and found a dish towel. I went back to the table and moved the deserted pasta into the still warm oven. Then I went out to the shed, found my left glove and the sharp hatchet, which I always hid in the low rafters of the woodshed so no one else would use it, and went to work on the wood. I didn't make much progress.

I sat down on the saw horse. It was an uncomfortable bench. I shifted my weight more to my feet, so the angled cross board did not press my flesh so sorely. But that was nothing to the pressure in my heart. Could the woman who lashed out so harshly at me and at her life, could she be the same person who, only this morning, had held an injured bird tenderly in her twisted hands and helped it fly again?

How could we be so cruel to each other? We each knew the other's vulnerable spot and headed for it like animals fighting for survival. Was that what we were doing? How could we survive? How could our marriage survive under such attack, such pressure, such lack of inner restraint? Had we now, in anger, fatally wounded ourselves? I knew I could not stay out there at the woodpile alone any longer. The questions in my heart urged me back to Elizabeth.

I gave up the pretense of chopping wood and with one glove and the hatchet in hand, walked around the house, past the roses and the patio and past the big window in our bedroom to the little hidden deck off our dressing room. It had been designed so we could come in directly from the garden to clean up without tracking all through the house.

Elizabeth was sitting there looking out toward the mountain. She seemed more to be looking into space than looking at the mountain or anything else. There was a single cigarette butt and four bent but unspent little matches and one dead one in the ceramic ashtray we had bought with left-over Italian currency at the airport in Rome. The opened package of cigarettes and the folder of matches were nearby. I came up onto the deck and sat down in the chair opposite her. I also looked out into space. There were no words spoken for a long painful time. I moved to put my glove and hatchet on the table. When I did so, Elizabeth picked up the cigarettes and matches. Was there no longer room for her things and my things in the same space? Or was it that her things would contaminate my things?

"Well?" she asked, tucking the cigarettes and matches into her sweater pocket.

"Well what?" I replied.

"Is this the end?" she asked.

"The end of what?"

"Of our marriage," she answered.

"Don't talk like that," I said.

We just sat there in the quiet of the early afternoon and looked at each other. Finally I said, "Please come sit in my lap." One delightful advantage to the difference in our height was the way Elizabeth could burrow down comfortably in my lap.

She didn't move for a long time. Then, without a word, she got up and came over and sat down carefully, stiffly, in my lap. It was more *on* my lap. She was still holding herself apart from me.

"I really mean it," she said. "I can't ask you to hang around just to take care of me and clean up my dirty ashtrays. I can't stand it when I see how burdened you are . . . and I know you want to be somewhere else . . . anywhere else . . . free to go . . . but here you are . . . stuck."

"There's nowhere else I want to be," I said. She did not reply at once. I really could not think of anywhere else I wanted to be. I wished our circumstances were different but they were ours and I did not want anyone else's. I did not feel martyred. I did feel trapped. But she was trapped also, only much more severely. She was quiet for such a long time that I thought she must be preparing a list of the places where she thought I would rather be. Maybe she was having a hard time with the list. She settled down a little further into my lap and rested her head on my chest.

After a few quiet moments which felt good to me, she said, "You could be traveling."

"Alone?" I asked.

"You could easily find someone. Stuart and Raezella have often invited us. They'd take you alone."

"You know I'm not going to do anything like that," I said with a slight edge in my voice.

"I just want you to feel free to go," she replied without conviction.

"Look, Elizabeth," I said with my words clearly spaced, "I regret more than anything that you are sick. But you are. There is nothing we can do about that. But as long as you are, there is really nothing else I want to do but to be with you and take care of you. It's no great sacrifice for me. There's nothing else I really want to do," I repeated slowly, emphatically. "Honestly. I've thought a lot about it."

"Even the dirty ashtrays?" she asked, seriously. Not joking.

"Oh, Lizzie, my love, even the dirty ashtrays. It was 'For better or worse,' wasn't it?" I asked with a cautious small smile. "I can't pretend I enjoy the 'worse' part. But it's worth it for the 'better' part. I'll manage the ashtrays and all the 'worse' you can offer, if you will forgive me for heckling you about the smoking. Sometimes I just can't help it."

"Then is it 'In sickness and health,' too?" she asked. "That was sick sick stuff I did today. It was just awful of me to go for a cigarette when you were screaming about my smoking. Forgive me, please. It's scary the hold they have on me."

"Oh yes, Lizzie, my love. 'In sickness and in health,' it is, indeed. In sickness and in health so long as we both shall live." I stopped. The words of death popped out. I quickly covered up. "Don't forget," I said, "even the sickness works both ways. You have handled far more bedpans for me than I have for you. Even an enema! Remember that horrible day? And the mess when the damn tube slipped? Repulsive! You have built up a lot of credit."

Elizabeth smiled tentatively and then replied, "Please don't joke." She settled even more deeply into my lap as though she would crawl inside me if she could. I was joyously relieved by our refreshed closeness, but she was getting heavy on my lap. It struck me funny and she saw my smile.

"What are you laughing at?" she asked.

"I was thinking that we are getting a little old for much lap-sitting," I bent over and kissed her ear. "You're getting heavy and my back is getting tired."

"It's so nice here," she said. "I'll get up in a minute." She paused and then became grave again. "That's just the point. Your back and my breath. Are we strong enough? I didn't do very well with the last bedpan, you may recall. If Frank Mueller hadn't come, you'd be on it yet . . . and the day may be coming when I can't even *begin* to get supper." She paused for a few moments. Then, very softly, looking down as though she were counting the buttons on my shirt, she said. "All day I have been worrying . . . I hate to say this, but . . . maybe I'm going to have to ask for the oxygen pretty soon. I was out of steam this morning by the time I got dressed."

The shift back to practical realities caught me off guard. I thought how little I sensed sometimes where she was coming from. "I really don't think the oxygen is going to be such a problem," I replied with more confidence than I felt. "They will tell us all about it and get us set up."

"But . . .," she stalled a moment before going on, "now . . . it's not only the oxygen that has me worried." Then looking up at me from her perch in my lap and tracing the outline of a heart with one finger around my face, she said very faintly, "I'm worried about us."

"Us?" I think we're just fine.

"After that fight?" she asked increduously.

"*Especially* after that fight," I answered. "That's probably the healthiest thing we've done about our marriage for months. When couples tell me they have come for pastoral counselling because they've just had an awful row, I tell them that may be the best start they could have toward a better relationship."

"If we came to you, sir pastor, for senior citizen marriage counselling, what would you tell us?" Elizabeth responded.

"I'd tell us to go find a qualified counsellor," I quipped.

"No, seriously, please," Elizabeth urged.

"I don't know. I've never thought about it."

"When I was sitting out here waiting for you to come find me, I had an inspiration," Elizabeth said, while letting me know, by shifting her weight away from me, that she had not forgotten her promise to abandon my lap. I helped her to her feet and smiled with empathy as I watched her shake out and recover from the cuddling before sitting down in her chair. "It occurred to me," she continued, "that maybe we have concentrated on me when we should have concentrated on us."

"Go on," I said. I knew right away that she was on to something crucial.

"I just wondered," she hesitated. "Well, it just seems to me sometimes that all we have thought and talked about for months is me and my heart and lungs, this curse I have . . . centered on that . . . tried to understand it and come to terms with it. And we have seldom ever thought or talked about what is happening to us, to our marriage, to our lives, and come to terms with that."

"We've probably thought a lot about it," I said, "but you are right. We have never *talked* about it. At least, not deliberately. But really that is what we did today."

"That was talk, all right," Elizabeth added.

"And it sure was about us,"' I said.

"But I hated it,"' Elizabeth shuddered. "I just hated it, every minute of it. A good fight is meant to be healthy now and then, but this felt dangerous, destructive. No thank you . . . no more fights like that, please."

"I suppose when you let the feelings all pile up . . . then when they explode, they can take over," I said. "It's then you say things you live to regret."

"So it's really important to talk regularly, isn't it?" Elizabeth added, "Even when you don't feel much like it . . . "

"Especially then," I added. Just at that moment I noticed a cloud of smoke rising from the lower reaches of Mt. St. Helena. "Look," I said, pointing to a slender spiral of smoke lifting straight up from a western slope of the mountain. "I hope somebody's in charge of that smoke."

CHAPTER 15

Exceeding Great and Precious Promises

The smoke lifted higher and higher in the windless sky. Had Mt. St. Helena become our Mt. Sinai where smoke went up like the smoke of a great kiln when the Lord descended upon it?

"It's a control burn," Elizabeth assured me. "There was a notice in the paper that the Forest Service would be burning several days this week if the wind permitted."

I welcomed the interruption. I had had enough 'talk' for one day. But I had the feeling that we had not finished. I was sure Elizabeth would not let it drop for long, but I wanted the credit for persisting.

"Good," I said. "Where were we? We were agreeing that it is important to talk even when we don't feel like it. Maybe by appointment. Every Wednesday at five. Something like that. At least, regularly, before there is time for a lot of bad stuff to build up."

"I've got it," said Elizabeth, delighted with her idea, "It's the 'control burn' of a well-managed marriage."

"'Control burn' . . . you're inspired," I responded enthusiastically. "That's really a wonderful metaphor. If you don't do some control burning, you'll end up with a forest fire."

"Like the one we just put out," Elizabeth added.

"Right. That's terrific. 'Control burn to save marriage.' Sounds like a headline from the tabloids. May I borrow it?"

"Thanks," she said. "But go easy. Remember only a madman or a fool starts a 'control burn' when there's a high wind blowing."

"Or for the fun of it," I added seriously. "Also, my dear creative one, the next time you are moaning and groaning about never having any original ideas, just remember that this was your idea, not mine."

"OK. I'll try. But come on now, let's have our first weekly 'control burn' right now," Elizabeth said. All the characteristic radiance was restored to her face. "It's safe now," she added, "the wind has all died down and I've got plenty to talk about." The metaphor was holding up!

"Remember it was you who asked for it," I chided her. Elizabeth often said that she sometimes didn't talk to me about her worries because I always came up with a solution. "Oh you and your solutions," she repeatedly breathed at me. She didn't get loud when she was teed-off; she just breathed the words out like escaping steam. "I don't want a solution. I just want you *to listen.*"

Remembering that repeated admonition, I continued, "I'm giving you fair warning because I think we *need* some solutions. I want more than talk in this 'control burn.' I want some 'How to' stuff, some practical suggestions, ideas . . . ideas for making the best, really the best, out of disappointment, out of the time we have left."

"I agree," Elizabeth responded cordially. "Don't forget your dear old Aunt Jennette."

"What about Aunt Jennette?"

"Oh you remember, the old family story about her and the man who kept jostling her on the subway and poking her with his packages. And she just smiled. Then later told you something to the effect that because you had told her it would just be a short ride she thought she should make it as pleasant as possible."

"Yes, but what about it?" I asked.

"I think that's about all the management we have managed these past months. There's been this unspoken agreement, 'If it's going to be such a short ride, let's make it as pleasant as we can!' And so far we've just slopped along . . . one crisis at a time. We never have really talked except in little pieces."

"That's right," I said, "but not only have we never talked much about what this is doing to our retirement but . . . "

Elizabeth interrupted, "Our retirement? It's not just our retirement, it is our marriage, our whole relationship."

"True, true," I went on, "it's not only that we've not talked about it, but we've acted as though we were helpless pawns, trapped. We've never bounced around any ideas of what we can do about it, what we can change, what we have some control over."

"In other words, be *intentional* about it," Elizabeth said. There was a rising note of questioning in her voice. Or was it a hint of scorn. 'Intentional' was one of my favorite words which she thought I overworked. "I've heard you talk endlessly about 'intentional marriage.' I know your whole spiel about it."

"Don't put it down 'til you've tried it," I said.

My response seemed to affect Elizabeth in a way I had not anticipated. "*I have tried it*," she said slowly and intensely, in a private fashion, as though she were ready to disclose a long hidden personal matter. As indeed, she was!

She went on, "Being married to you has taken a lot more than 'intentionality'! That's just your fancy word for good intentions. Well, I learned long ago where good intentions lead."

"Would you prefer bad intentions," I said defensively.

"No, my love, you know better than that. But making a marriage work takes more than good intentions . . . something behind them or under them . . . holding them up."

"Like what?" I asked.

"Like keeping promises," she said quietly without hesitation. Turning and looking straight at me, she went on. "I learned about promises from my parents, from my childhood church, that Baptist church in that insignificant little town in Georgia where they may not sing much Bach but where a promise is a promise come hell or high water! What do you think I was doing in those miserable years in New Haven when you would have been glad if I had taken my children and disappeared? I intended to make that marriage work. I was determined because I had promised. I had made a promise before God and you and the children. It was going to work . . . in spite of you, if necessary. You call me stubborn."

"'Committed' sounds nicer," I interjected.

"Have it your own way," Elizabeth went on with hardly a pause. She was not through. "You know you really hurt me once, put me down. I've never forgotten."

She paused as though the recollection of it brought more pain than she had anticipated. "What on earth are you talking about?" I asked.

"When we were having all that trouble, you said that I just didn't want to go back to Georgia. That infuriated me! It still rankles! Is there something wrong with not wanting to be defeated, not wanting to break your promise, not wanting to give up on your love?"

There was an acute silence between us. I wondered if this "control burn" was getting out of hand. It had been many years since either one of us had mentioned the difficulties we had endured in the first years of our marriage. We had grown far beyond all that in the fulfillment we had found in California. I had largely forgotten how unhappy we were . . . and how resolute she was! It wasn't a pleasant recollection. At that time, I had seen her determination as my enemy. I have since learned that many blended families have a rough time the first few years. If someone isn't committed beyond his or her own pleasure, the newly formed family can easily go down the drain.

Finally I said, "I never thought before how lucky I am that you took our vows so literally . . . so bindingly. That's an awful awkward word, 'bindingly.' But that is what it takes. You supplied enough 'bind' for both of us, thank the good Lord."

"And how lucky I am," Elizabeth quickly countered, for she wasn't through yet, "that the preacher didn't ask you if you loved me."

"But I did love you," I protested.

"Oh, no you didn't. Not in the romantic sense. Not in the orange blossoms and Robert Browning sense. Do you realize that you never called me 'Liz' or 'Lizzie' until we came to California? I'm afraid I knew you didn't love me as I wanted and needed to be loved all those long months before. But I trusted your intentions . . . promises."

I got up and knelt down by the chair. "I could never have loved you then as I love you now," I whispered to her as I took her hands in mine.

"But does it always have to be so rough in order to be good eventually," Elizabeth replied with a wistfulness in her voice that felt as though she were thirty-nine again sitting on the rocks below the lighthouse at Pemaquid, New Harbour, Maine, June 1957.

"Maybe. I don't know," I answered. "But, Liz, my love, you've gotten me on my knees at last. You are right about *part* of all that. I *was* unsure about romantic love, about sex. And don't blame it on the poor Puritans. They wanted 'purity' of doctrine but they loved to bundle. We could better blame Victoria for our inhibitions. And I had plenty! But I knew you really stirred me. No doubt about that. But passion can be ephemeral."

"How did you ever find the courage to go through with it . . . and marry this frightful person?" Elizabeth said with more than a hint of sarcasm!

"Don't do that, please! How can we be honest with each other if we get defensive," I pled.

"Forgive me, please," she said. "I do appreciate your candor. But how did you go through with it?"

"I'm not sure," I replied wistfully, slowly. "I remember how panicky I was driving with your father over to the church. I remember the bridge between the village and the church. When we drove over it, I thought it was too late to turn back. Then I looked at your Dad. He was so steady and loving. Your family, the Maine cottage, the jokes and concerns about the church . . . it all was familiar, it was like my family, and I felt safe trusting myself and my children to you and them. I felt safe getting committed to you even if my emotions were in a mess. See how wise the Church is in what it asks couples. See what I would have missed if certainty about love rather than promises to a person were required at the altar."

"What would you have missed?" Elizabeth asked.

"I would have missed the most beautiful part of my life . . . you, you, Liz, you and the love we have now, grown-up love, that has blossomed out of promises, promises kept."

Elizabeth bent over and kissed the top of my head very softly. "Thank you. You are sweet and generous. But it works both ways," she said.

"Both ways?" I asked, looking up at her and wondering how long my knees and back would hold out.

"Yes, both ways," she replied with a quiet steady voice which made clear she was not arguing with me, only stating a fact. "Promises grow out of love, too. I think that is what every woman wants. Love. Then the promises." She looked at me deeply and then added with a gentle laugh, "But better late than never with the love."

And as she spoke I heard the voice of a much younger woman who looked at me that summer afternoon, sitting on the enormous rock we had claimed as our own at Pemaquid. She looked at me, whom she scarcely knew, and responded clearly and without any hint of hesitation of any sort, "Browne, I love you, too." She said it with almost no idea at all of what the promises, which would surely follow, would involve. It was the love she felt which reinforced her promises. It was the promises I had made which reinforced my love. Maybe it was the best possible combination for a marriage that had to grow in very thin and rocky soil.

"I think I had it one way and you had it the other," Elizabeth said. "I was crushed when it finally dawned on me that the promise was stronger for you than the love. It was the other way for me, I thought. It feels odd to me to hear you say that you always felt the promise was so strong in me. But it takes some of both. The balance may differ. Maybe it always does. Maybe that's the best way. Differences attract."

"But you can overdo the differences," I said. "To be sure, without the promises, I would never have found the love. But, never forget, if there had not been some awareness of the love, I'd never have made the promises."

"Everyone is saying these days that we should celebrate our differences in a democracy," Elizabeth said.

"But we're talking about marriage. Haven't you found out it's no democracy! Next time we get married to anyone, I think we need to get some of the differences under control," I said laughing. "I think it would be more useful to require a basal metabolism test than a blood test. Wouldn't it be great if we were both night persons, instead of you wanting to stay up all night and me konking out at dusk. It'd be so much easier to keep our promises."

"I don't agree," Elizabeth said. "If we were both night people who would bounce out of bed in the morning and get the coffee?"

"And if we were both morning people," I answered, willing to play this game, "who would be ready for fun at night?"

"Are you trying to tell me you are ready to go to bed?" she asked.

"It's the middle of the day!" I replied.

"What's that got to do with it?" she laughed.

I had long since got up off my knees, but I was still gazing at her. I smiled at her question. What a remarkable woman, I thought, but is she saying that in order to reassure me that she is still up to a good romp in the bed? This was one worry I had been having that I was not about ready to bring to the "control burn" hour.

"Act your age," I jokingly chided her.

"That's exactly what I'm doing," she answered.

"What other good news do you have?" I asked.

"That I still remember your Aunt Jennette."

"How's that?"

"Isn't that clear?" she responded with her whole face alight with teasing and love. "If it's going to be such a short ride, it shouldn't be unpleasant."

I pulled her to her feet and kissed her deeply. We stood there together for a long time, holding each other in the bond of passion which we never knew when we were younger. After a long time I took her by the hand and led her to the bedroom.

"This is the only time I don't think that big window is such a good idea," she said.

* * * * * * * *

Later that day—it was actually almost dinner time but it was still technically a Wednesday afternoon—I took down the great ship's bell we had brought from Maine and hit it a couple of times with a tack hammer, the only instrument I could find.

"What's all the noise about?" Elizabeth called from the screened porch where she was reading the *Audubon* magazine which we found in the morning's mail when we got around to it.

"Time for 'control burn' hour," I said.

"I thought we already had it for today," she answered.

"No way. That was just preparation. I have more to say."

"Oh no," she groaned, as she put the magazine aside, and I sat down in the other comfortable chair.

"I've just been thinking that we ought to write up a service for married persons to renew their marriage vows when they retire."

"I bet it will be full of 'intentional' verbs," Elizabeth said.

"Intentional verbs? "I asked.

"Isn't that what we were talking about earlier. 'Will you do this? Is it your intention to do that . . . love, honor, obey?' Well, skip the obey."

"Oh, that. Sure. I think it still holds. Maybe even more when you are old."

"And sick?" Elizabeth asked in a whisper I might have missed.

"Yes. I suppose so," I replied.

"Count me out then," she said. "I don't want you caring for me because you promised to do so years ago. I could only accept it if it was offered because you love me now."

I felt she was right. And I knew she meant it. For all her talk about keeping promises, she only wanted promises kept because of love.

"Well, if you write up such a service," Elizabeth said, "I hope you'll limber up a bit and use inclusive language and be realistic."

"Like so?" I asked.

Elizabeth picked it right up, "Like 'Do you promise to dress up for each other at least once a day? Well, once a week, at least? or read the same book, or bring home a flower, or bake a cake once every decade! or stay out of each other's hair?"

"What about your 'control burn' hour?" I asked.

"That, too," Elizabeth added. "Do you promise to get all your gripes out every Wednesday afternoon at four o'clock?"

"It could get to be a very long session. We old folks would worry about missing the Early Bird Special," I suggested, gently ribbing Elizabeth about Denny's economy meals.

But my words sailed right past her. She was momentarily stopped at another point. "But what about all the good intentions, all the promises we make that we don't keep . . . some we find we . . . we cannot keep," she said very soberly.

"Of course. We're human beings. Not perfect. Not even as strong as we sometimes believe. That's why marriages have to have lots of give and take."

Elizabeth wasn't satisfied. "But what about those promises," she pressed, "the ones we break that break us, too. The ones we make with such good intent, but can't keep?"

"Such as?" I asked stupidly.

There was a stretched-out silence. Finally Elizabeth said, with a faraway look in her eyes, a look full of sadness and gentleness, her eyes so full, so heavy, they could not turn and look at me, "How can I keep the promise I made to care for you 'in sickness and in health,' when I can't even strike a match?"

I reached out to her in silence and looked at her and finally said, "None of us can do all we want to do . . . all that would be good to do . . . because we're finite creatures . . . sometimes we just can't. We are limited, mortal beings. That's far more important to confess to each other, as well as to God, and to ourselves, too, which may be the hardest of all, . . . that is a lot more important confession than to admit that we left the top off the toothpaste after promising we wouldn't."

Elizabeth smiled. "You always make me feel better. But finite or not, I think we should try. I think we should keep our promises if we possibly can. Otherwise they don't mean anything."

"Of course," I said, "but to fail is not the end of the line. God is the one who doesn't fail. Not us. That's pretty central to being God. It doesn't seem to be a characteristic of human beings . . . not to fail."

"OK." Elizabeth said, apparently more content. "But now," she continued, "if you and God will get down to earth, I want to ask you—and Her," she grinned playfully for a passing moment, "what we can do to back up our promises, even the ones we can't fully keep? What can we do to have a good marriage in sickness and in health when we are too sick to do what comes naturally?"

"What are you getting at?" I asked. "For example?" I was beginning to suspect I was in the process of being lovingly trapped.

"Money, for example," Elizabeth said.

Oh, dear God, I thought, here we go, but I said, "Well, sex after lunch so it's gotta be money before dinner."

"Well, we've talked a lot about intention," Elizabeth said. "And it often takes money to back up intention . . . even good intentions."

"OK. So what?"

Elizabeth continued. "We've been saving for our old age. Maybe now that everything's changed—except our age—we should take another look at our savings. Maybe we can use them to . . . . "

"To refinance our marriage?" I filled in.

"Well, I'm not ready to spend our savings just to save our marriage," Elizabeth laughed. "Get your priorities straight! But let's do take another look at our budget."

"For instance?" I asked.

"All right," she replied. "I'd like not to worry about the telephone bill when I call Berkeley or the kids. So lets just plan on . . . really *intend* to pay lots more to Pacific Bell every month."

"That's fine with me," I said. "And how about spending some of the travel money on household help? I know I promised to do the vacuuming even before you got sick. And here goes another promise. But that's harder work than cutting the grass. As a house cleaner, I'm dragging my butt."

"Why didn't you say so?" Elizabeth chided. "I would even find money in the back of the check book for that."

"I got out of that easier than I thought," I beamed. "Also, if we're going to be 'intentional' about these years, I think we must sign a solemn agreement about this 'control burn' business. Regular time and place. It won't work if we wait until we're in a crisis. I really didn't realize we weren't being honest with each other."

"Come off it," Elizabeth scoffed, "where have you been? No one is honest with a sick person. Hardly anyone anyway. And if you can't be honest with me, we're in for a bad time."

"Not honest with you?" I asked.

"That's not quite true. You are, most of the time. But you weren't being honest with me about doing the cleaning. I guess it is mostly other people who have trouble with being honest with someone who is handicapped in any way. All in the name of kindness. Protective love? It feels more like protective insults!"

"Is that what we found out about ourselves? A problem with honesty?" I asked. "For years I have heard retired people say that their problem is because they are together all the time. And they are driving each other crazy with their togetherness. But actually they are only in the same space. They are not 'together'."

"How do you get 'together'?" Elizabeth asked.

"The same way you keep honest?"

"How's that?" Elizabeth asked.

"Control burn, of course!" I said.

"But it won't work if we wait until we have a big hot forest fire," Elizabeth warned. "I really thought you enjoyed vacuuming. I thought you felt that now the house would really be clean and tidy . . . at least once a week! Unchecked assumptions all ready to take off and do a lot of damage."

"Let's agree," I said. "Every Wednesday afternoon. At the Happy Hour until further notice? We shouldn't have had to have a fight in order for you to tell me how much my hovering was bugging you."

The air was cleared. I think we were both excited about our expressed intention. If this was to be such a short ride, we had announced to each other our promise that it shouldn't be unpleasant. And that was largely up to us.

But that was only part of the truth. It was not altogether up to us whether we liked it or not. We had a great company of family and friends who were also resolved that this short ride should be as pleasant for us as they could help to make it. And just recently young Dr. Mueller had been added to that roster of determined friends.

CHAPTER 16

Friends Who Stick Closer
than a Brother

Dr. Mueller's management of Elizabeth's illness required fairly regular visits to his office. Sometimes she would need to go every week or oftener. At other times, three or four weeks would pass before another visit. Increasingly we organized our lives around those appointments. In the early months, she drove in by herself. Then for a while, I chauffeured her but waited in the car. I was always eager for a report and she tried to tell me everything he had said.

"Next time," she said one day after an appointment, "you come with me. I'd much prefer to have you hear everything first hand. It will make it easier for us to talk it over." Dr. Mueller encouraged me to do so, recognizing that we were in this together. As the months passed, I often accepted the invitation. Later on my services were required to help with the oxygen tank. One of the consequences of these three-way sessions was that we became good friends with Frank Mueller.

From the beginning he called her Elizabeth. But Elizabeth and I, reared as we were in an earlier generation, called him Dr. Mueller. I noticed that he didn't call me much of anything. Then one day around Christmas our phone rang and I responded.

"Browne, this is Frank Mueller." It took me a moment to regain my equilibrium. "Angie and I wondered if you and Elizabeth would like to join us next Friday night. We are having a few friends in for a holiday bash."

We had turned a corner in our relationship. Elizabeth wasn't able to go to the party, but I did. I met the young doctor's wife, Angela, a fresh and fair young woman with a tint of fire in her hair. I saw a very tiny baby girl sleeping through the party and a four-year-old girl peeping at the people. Our titles and our disparate ages alike were lost in the warmth of their home. I also learned that Frank Mueller liked to cook and to eat. Maybe we had more in common, despite the difference in our ages, than I thought.

A few weeks later I was pleased when Elizabeth suggested we should invite them to dinner. She had become my tutor in the kitchen and was having a wonderful time confronting me with recipes she heard on Narsai David and Harvey Steinman's popular San Francisco radio cooking school. She organized her weekday morning not to miss a session. If she were going to be my cooking teacher, she vowed one day, she was going to teach me things I would never learn from reading Fanny Farmer!

In the midst of prolonged deliberations about what food we would serve the Muellers, Elizabeth said, "You know very well that I would never experiment with guests, but inasmuch as you seem untroubled by any such modesty, here's just the thing for you to try on the Muellers. Narsai gave out the recipe this morning. 'Hot smoked sturgeon on a bed of cabbage, bacon and onion.'"

"You're joking," I replied. "You know I don't like cabbage and have never smoked anything in my whole long impressive career as a cook."

"I dare you," she said.

That was all it took. I couldn't get sturgeon and settled for halibut which was a mistake. It fell apart and we lost most of it in the fire when Frank tried to help me serve it up. The others assured me that the cabbage was about as good as cabbage can be. But Frank informed me that for him it was worse than beans in its capacity to produce an embarrassing response. Nonetheless it was a nourishing evening in important ways.

I was impressed by the important role that food played in establishing a deeper relationship with the Muellers. "Breaking bread together" doesn't have to be in the church. It was also true with John and Karen Mitchell. We returned their hospitality one night when Elizabeth was still doing most of the cooking. I was glad of that for I did not want to cook for Karen Mitchell who is honored in culinary circles quite beyond these neighboring small towns of Calistoga and St. Helena.

Elizabeth had a knack with pie crust. I have never been able to match it. If I get it rich and tender and flaky, I can't handle it. It falls apart. The night the Mitchells came to dinner Elizabeth served lemon pie for dessert. Later she received a beautiful note from John Mitchell. He said he wanted to write the thank you note because he didn't want Karen to know how much he had enjoyed the lemon pie. Like his mother's!

These beautiful younger friends moved gracefully back and forth across generational lines. They possessed the directness and spontaneity to relate to us as persons. We felt they liked us for ourselves. We had another younger friend, or family of friends, Amador Diaz, his father, and his brothers. When Amador could not come to help me in the vegetable garden or stack the wood for winter heat, he would always see that Pablo or Juan or Miguel or Guillermo or Gilberto or their genial father came in his place. These young men were unfailingly honest and prompt and clean and loving.

I know our absent sons grew admittedly jealous of Amador who did practical chores for us which they longed to do for us themselves. Our four children, who had come together into a new family thirty years before in Maine, were now full of their own responsibilities in places as distant as the Canadian border and West Berlin. Yet no year of Elizabeth's illness passed without each one of them, as well as her sister, Gayner, from Georgia, spending at least a week with her and lamenting the duties and distances which separated us.

Perhaps it was in part because of the long absences of our own children that Elizabeth found such incredible joy in this trinity of younger friends who were living their lives right here with us, a Roman Catholic physician, a Vietnam hero contractor, and a strong young Mexican. These relationships deepened in joy and intimacy as we sensed how they worried with us as Elizabeth grew more and more limited. One time I discovered John Mitchell, unannounced, working at the outdoor faucets where we connected hoses to water the flowers.

"What the devil are you doing?" I asked him. He had some old-fashioned porcelain faucet handles which he was installing. "You are really carrying this antique stuff to the extreme. Who wants white porcelain handles that read 'hot' or 'cold' on their outdoor faucets?"

Mitchell looked at me with a hint of exasperation. "You do," he replied quietly. "They give some leverage. I think Elizabeth will be able to turn them on and off."

When Amador finished his work, he never left without coming to the door to find Elizabeth. He would tell her good-bye in a way that seemed to say, "Now please don't be lonely till I come back next Saturday." One time when Elizabeth called Frank about a problem and he thought he should see her at his office promptly but I was not home to bring her into town and she no longer was driving, he found someone to come and get her and take her home.

It is also curious and instructive that each of these three caring and more intimate relationships did not come through church or club or neighborhood. Each one came through a daily vocation, compassionately exercised: physician, carpenter, gardener. Protestant theologians should be irate at the increasing assumption that one must be ordained to engage in a Christian vocation. The ghosts of Luther and Calvin must tremble at such heresy!

Loneliness and the absence of intimacy threaten to dry up life especially for the ill and the aging. Philip Slater's book *The Pursuit of Loneliness* is subtitled, "American Culture at the Breaking Point." His thesis, as I recall it, is that human loneliness in large cities and in little towns is a pervasive disease in American life, pounding at it in many forms and bringing it to the breaking point.

Certainly it would have been the breaking point for us if we had been allowed to use Elizabeth's illness as an excuse for us not to make new friends or nourish old ones. I have observed older couples, retired, perhaps new in town, seeking some excuse to withdraw and to be spared the effort of remaining a responsible part of the human community. "We've done our share," they say. "Now it's someone else's turn."

People who find it necessary to move to adult communities must take pains not to be trapped there outside the broader world. Responsible citizens living in such monolithic communities report difficulty in resisting the assumption that when one retires from daily work, one also retires from public responsibility. There are many who do resist that mindset and they become the larger town's greatest asset, persons with skills and time to devote to the larger community, including children and youth.

Withdrawal into a life of entertainment and travel is sad to see at any time in American life but especially grievous when the hope for our future lies in making our diversity a strength in our communities and not a threat to them. Older people have a particular responsibility to appreciate and nourish that diversity which includes diversity in age as well as in ethnic backgrounds.

It is a great temptation to divest oneself of every responsibility possible in illness and in age. That is not only a loss to the larger community but it may aggravate the illness and speed the aging of both soul and body. In retrospect I know that our marriage and our spirit would never have grown and thrived during the years of Elizabeth's illness if we had been allowed to do that.

I say "if we had been allowed to do that" because we were members of a "little family of the heart," which, by its very nature as a persistent and loving community, was determined that we should not. They were friends, an innumerable company who would not let us escape from their caring.

Slater contends that one human desire frustrated by our Western culture is "the desire for community—the wish to live in trust and fraternal cooperation with one's fellows in a total and visible collective entity." That is what the parish church had been for us in Berkeley. We had come to call it "the little family of the heart." For us it was the family which every person needs. To go to church was to meet with people who loved you, warts and all.

We were amazed to note that the characteristics which Virginia Satir, a famed student of family life, found in her research to mark vital and nurturing families, such as good communication and being linked to society in an open and hopeful way, are qualities which mark vital and nurturing parishes. To go to church on Sunday morning was not, for us, an irksome duty but an anticipated and refreshing homecoming. It was also more than that. It was to join with other human beings in affirming a common faith in a transcendent Power who is persistent in forgiving, and to experience the breakthrough of that forgiveness.

Without forgiveness tomorrow is simply a projection of yesterday with an ever increasing load of its garbage which we can't dispose of by our own effort. Broken promises, for instance, and everything else we ought not to have done or failed to do or be. The absence of true intimacy and the presence of penetrating loneliness seem inevitable to me for those who do not know the release which forgiveness brings, both human and divine.

I have trouble with any religion which lays a guilt trip on people instead of lifting a guilt trip from them. What if we left church or synagogue week after week poignantly aware, as Jews and Christians must be, of the pain of the world and our reasonable responsibility about it, but nonetheless feeling deeply forgiven, hence re-energized for participation in life. Forgiven, as Norman Cousins said in one of the last things he wrote, so "the blocks to our preceptions, our prospects, and our pleasures are removed."

If Elizabeth and I learned nothing else in the battles we had with ourselves and with each other through these years, we learned that without forgiveness it is impossible to live in intimacy with one another or with other people or, Elizabeth would add, with the whole creation! So the persistent love and forgiveness Elizabeth and I knew in and through "the little family of the heart" provided the context in which life could be enlarging and beautiful even as it seemed to be shutting down.

Thus it was when we first left Berkeley and had many weekends free to spend in the country, we started our search for a church nearby. On the Sunday when the new minister came to the Berkeley church, we listened to the broadcast service at 10 o'clock. In order to get the station clearly we had to get in the car and drive twenty miles or so into the Napa Valley. The congregation gave a rousing and supportive and laughing, loving welcome to the new pastor and we realized that we really had left and must not intrude upon or harm this new relationship of pastor and people.

We were both homesick as we drove aimlessly around listening to the service. We realized how easily a former pastor can allow her or his feelings to hinder the work of the successor. Regret and envy and jealousy can easily take root. See again, how much forgiveness is needed to keep life moving ahead!

Soon it was almost eleven o'clock and we decided it was time to stop feeling sorry for ourselves. By that time we were in St. Helena and decided "to try out" the Presbyterian Church there. It was small but had long given good support to the seminary where I was then working. The exterior of the simple carpenter gothic church looked cared for. Once we were inside we felt at home. There was a sense of energy with colorful banners and sincere warmth in the welcome at the door. But more, it was a people gathered in a place to worship Almighty God and soon we were joining with them in the prayer of confession and the Kyrie and in hearing the assurance of forgiveness and acceptance.

When at last the beautifully crafted small baroque organ spilled over with the Gloria, we were drawn to our feet and found ourselves praising God with God's people. They didn't know it yet, but new members of their "little family of the heart" were being born in that instant. We were embarking on a tomorrow which was not just a hopeless endless backward-looking repetition of yesterday. A new little family was found, not to replace the former one, but to supplement it and to multiply our riches in friendship and forgiveness. In many ways it was refreshingly different from the Berkeley church: for example, at that precise moment the pastor, Roswell Gordon, was sailing with two friends in a small craft from the Golden Gate to Hawaii! A daring venture. We were in for pastoral care with a flair.

CHAPTER 17

Better to Marry than to Burn

When I was the young and inexperienced pastor of a New England congregation I made a hospital call on an old man, a widower. He was 75! Younger than I now am! He was facing a serious operation. He told me that he had made a bargain with the Lord and had promised ten thousand dollars to the church building fund if he survived the operation.

"It's really important to you to live, isn't it?" I said.

"It sure is," he responded, "haven't you heard?"

"Heard what?"

"That woman I met in Florida last winter."

"Yes. You introduced me to her last summer."

His steely blue eyes lit up as he whispered to me, "We are going to get married if I live."

I hope I was appropriately enthusiastic not only about his marriage but about his recovery, for now, as pastor of his church, I had a vested interest in his health. Ten thousand dollars. Yes! But marriage? At 75!

Finally I said to him, "How do you feel about it?" I meant to inquire about the whole idea of getting married, moving, making changes at 75. He apparently thought the "it" was making love.

"I feel just as excited and eager and in love as I did at 25."

I must have blushed. I was not about to initiate a conversation about sex with a 75-year-old parishioner or any other! The idea that he might have sexual desire was excluded from my

109

brain like some impossibility that was immoral even to contemplate. And "in love"? A senior adult might have a friendly and practical marriage, if it didn't cost too much Social Security, but "in love"?

"That's all right," he said. "If you live long enough you will understand."

And I have lived long enough to understand!

He did recover. He did marry. The church did get the ten thousand dollars. He lived into his nineties. As I became good friends with him and his wife I learned that they enjoyed each other deeply in every way, a profound relationship of body and soul.

If it's going to be "such a short ride, it might as well be pleasant!"

So it is that loneliness and intimacy have a public side. But they also have a gracefully hidden and precious private side. They are appropriately out of public view and therefore the pain and disappointment which they can sometimes bring often go unrecognized. Some of the problems of private intimacy which couples face as they grow older or when one of them is ill or physically handicapped are not readily resolved.

Elizabeth and I both knew that her illness and my anxiety about it had put us into a delicate circumstance. She feared she was no longer attractive and I feared that she would over reach herself in order to please me. We talked openly about the bind we were in and the disappointment we were suffering, but neither of us could be really objective and candid about our feelings and our failures.

One morning as I got out of bed and struggled into my bathrobe I said to Elizabeth without turning to look at her, "I think I'd better find a sex surrogate." I didn't expect her to say much, but I did expect her to say *something*. She said nothing. She just lay there in the bed. My unease grew with the moment. I expected her to support me and help me go about this new project.

Minutes, hours, eons passed. And she said nothing. Nothing at all! Finally I sat back down on my side of the bed and turned to her. "Well," I said, "what about it?"

"I didn't think I was that bad," she said into the covers.

"It's not you. It's me," I urged.

"But isn't that a rather drastic solution?" she asked.

"What's drastic about that?" I replied. "Lots of people do it."

"You don't know anyone who ever did that," she said.

"Of course, I do. Lots of people. You'd be surprised. They don't talk about it much. But they get lots of help."

"Well, don't ask me," she said. "I don't want to hear anything about it. In fact, if you do . . . "

"If I do, . . . what?" I repeated.

She didn't reply. Finally she said, "But how would you go about it? Would you ask Frank?"

"Never," I said. "I don't want anyone to know."

"I should hope not," she said with the disappointment of disgrace in her voice.

"Oh don't carry on so," I said with a bit of irritation. "Don't make a big thing out of it. Just the other day in her column Ann Landers gave the address of a place you can write which will send you a list of them in your area."

"You're crazy," Elizabeth said. "You're out of your head. The newspaper wouldn't print anything like that even if Ann Landers had it in her column."

"She did, too. I saved it and I wrote in for the list."

"A list of sex surrogates? I can't believe my ears," Elizabeth sat straight up in bed as though she had received a tremendous poke from somewhere under the mattress. She was fully awake and alert. "Sex surrogates! That's illegal. I really won't . . ."

"Who said anything about sex surrogates?" I replied.

"You did."

"I did not."

"You most certainly did. If not, then what has this whole insane conversation been about?"

"I said I wanted to find a sex therapist."

"Oh dear God," wheezed Elizabeth, one not usually given to anything bordering on the profane.

"I just didn't want to ask Frank to recommend one. There must be several certified marriage and sex therapists around here somewhere."

Elizabeth began to laugh. I went around to her side of the bed and sat down. "Surrogate?" I said. "I'm glad to see how I can get a rise out of you."

"What a fright," she said. "I think it's a good idea. Maybe he can persuade you that I won't break just because I can't always breathe!"

"He or she," I said.

"I draw the line," Elizabeth replied, "No 'shes'."

Several weeks later I received a printout of all the certified sex therapists on the West coast. There were several nearby. You couldn't tell much by the list. Only what academic degree they had earned and that they were certified by the authorized association. Usually you could make a pretty good guess as to their sex. You could tell if any on the list shared offices with any of the others by their addresses. Nonetheless, I thank Ann Landers for the service. Or was it Miss Manners?

I chose two to investigate. The first one I called was away on vacation. Through his machine he invited me to leave a message. He sounded a bit unctuous to me. Besides, I was nervous and didn't know quite what to say. So I hung up without leaving any message. Then I tried my second choice. He had a machine also. This time I responded and left a call. He returned the call and invited me to come in and have a preliminary interview. It was clear that I would be interviewing him as well as he would be interviewing me.

In a few days I went for the appointment. I deliberated for a long time whether or not to wear a necktie, jeans or slacks, shoes or boots! From the first moment I was glad I was with him. There began a long and liberating relationship with Richard E. Levy, Ph.D., marriage and family counsellor.

It was not long before he helped me understand some of the problems we were having. I would race home and share them with Elizabeth and she would say (sometimes), "That is exactly what I've been telling you." Other times she would say, "That's a lot of nonsense." We would argue and discuss and experiment.

Elizabeth was reared in a household which was less secretive about sex than mine. We began to understand that we are part of a generation full of abused persons, having suffered the abuse of silence about sex which can be more damning sometimes than physical abuse. We learned how much the malignant skirts of Victoria had shadowed our days. We wept to think that it was only at the end of life that we had come to experience the greatest joy and pleasure in our consummation, soul *and* body. We mourned for many other people, especially older people, whose deeply ingrained problems keep them from seeking help . . . not, thank you, of a sex surrogate, but of a counsellor, a therapist, professionally prepared to help human beings understand their total sexuality and to experience genuine physical intimacy which is much much more than just sexual intercourse, and can be intensely experienced without it.

Dr. Levy helped me understand much of what Elizabeth had been trying to tell me. Most of all, I suppose, was the conflict and confusion in expectations because we had different understandings of intimacy. But he helped us in practical ways, too. We learned simple schemes to get around the presence of the oxygen tank and the tubing when they became our constant companions. We experienced closeness of a deeply nurturing kind which did not depend upon sexual performance. Most of all, we learned to talk and communicate in other ways more clearly and trustingly. During many months, as the darkness deepened in our lives, Richard Levy gave me support and encouragement quite beyond my initial goal. He helped Aunt Jennette's sunny motto come to life, although I doubt she ever thought of it in *this* connection! "If it's going to be such a short ride, it might as well be pleasant." Indeed!

CHAPTER 18

Eating the Bread of Idleness

We had gotten our act together just in time. For the very next day after my first session with Dr. Levy, more than a year after the pulmonary specialist had mentioned oxygen to Elizabeth, it was clear that she could not postpone it any longer. Here was another major adjustment for us to face. Frank made the arrangements with a home health care company to install the equipment. It was not many days before their white panelled van with the green diamond sign hanging low on the front bumper began regular visits in our driveway.

Elizabeth was very much interested in the mechanics of the oxygen equipment. From the first moment that she placed the tubing over her ears and around her face and into her nostrils she wore it as naturally as a pair of eyeglasses. She was smoking very very little these days and the oxygen helped her in that battle. But at home she was so unaware of the tubing to which she was tied that one day she all but struck a match to light a cigarette before she came to! Once in a while she fussed when the tube caught in a doorway or tugged unpleasantly at her face. The oxygen she had resisted and which we felt would add another irksome strain to our lives came, at last, not as an unwelcomed intruder but as a welcomed friend. It not only eased her breathing but gave her more energy.

A technician came the first time to teach us how to use the equipment. There was a machine about 18 inches square which we located between the kitchen and the bedroom. It made the oxygen out of the air in the room and fed it to Elizabeth through a 50-foot plastic hose. It is amazing how much of a house can be covered in fifty feet radiating in all directions. There was no worry unless the power failed. When the oxygen providers learned how unreliable the power was in our valley, they brought an immense tank with a three day supply of oxygen and stood it in the corner of the living room. We seldom had to shift to it, but when the power went off in the middle of the night, it was not long before Elizabeth was awake with distress and we were glad for that huge sentinel standing in the corner of the living room. Despite its welcomed comfort, the arrival of the oxygen equipment also slashed a heavy mark on the calendar of our short ride together. "I went almost a year without it," Elizabeth said brightly on the first day after the installer had left. "Dr. Solomon said it would add two years to my life so I guess we have two still to go."

We both knew, although neither one of us said so, that we would never again be together without its company. Its constant hum was the sound of life and on the few occasions when the electricity failed and the hum stopped, it was like the soundlessness of death.

There were also small portable green tanks. These lifted easily into the car and it was not long before Elizabeth needed one if we were to be gone from home more than a few minutes. For several months Elizabeth was reluctant to go out in public using the oxygen except in the car where the tank was inconspicuous. Her resistance cut seriously into our social life. Ever since we had rebudgeted for a life anchored to home and doctor, we had been enjoying meeting friends for dinner in one of the many restaurants which grace the Napa Valley. It felt to me like an unnecessary narrowing of our life to give up such outings. I resented her resistance. When I realized how strong my feelings were, I was glad that we were committed to a regular "control burn" session every week whether either of us asked for it or not. So I brought it up at the next session which we often combined with the "Happy Hour." Maybe the "Happy Hour" facilitated the "control burn" part of the "engagement"!

"Look here," I said, "you may dread being seen in restaurants with that green tank, but I'd like it. I'm sure we'd get better service." She laughed and agreed to try it out once with good friends, Kay and Bob Riddell. We made the date for dinner without mentioning that it was a test case. Those wonderful friends handled the situation with such nonchalance and impeccable tact that the issue was laid to rest that night. I was grateful. Elizabeth discovered she could manage the risk of strange faces turned momentarily in her direction.

The immaculately dressed and well-mannered young men who the home health care company always appeared to have in endless supply to make deliveries were another curiosity for us. They looked as though they all met the same requirements, medium size, well-groomed hair, starched clean casual clothes, and an occasional earring suggesting the hint of repressed non-conformity. They were so well drilled in their duties and so proper and polite in their conversation and so absolutely antiseptic in their coming and going, we began to wonder if they were robots. We also wondered what they thought. One time when one of these careful young men was checking out the system, Elizabeth said to him, "Well, I've made it for another two weeks. Are you surprised?" The employees' training manual had not prepared the tidy young man for that question.

"Yes, mam," he said. And then added, "I mean . . . uh, so I see." He became so flustered by his unrehearsed reply that Elizabeth was touched.

"Don't let me tease you," she said. "I intend to be here long after you've been promoted to the home office."

* * * * * * * *

The oxygen was kind to us. It seemed to bring Elizabeth up to a higher energy level than she had known for a long time. Even Abby, the indoor cat, regarded the little machine and its constant hum as a friend. When Elizabeth's lap was not available, she would settle down on the rug next to it. Elizabeth gradually increased the hours she used the oxygen and so remained pretty constant in feeling better. But it was not many months until she was very uncomfortable without it even long enough to take a shower. Nonetheless, with its help she was pleased to enjoy time in the kitchen again. The long tubing cooperated except around the refrigerator where it frequently got entangled. Elizabeth would just back up and free it and go on as though that was to be expected. More than a year later she was still getting some of the meals started. Once in a while she would last long enough to finish the entire preparation. But I usually had to be ready to take over.

We had both taken our "intentional" plan seriously for her to teach me how to cook. Most of the time she enjoyed it. I am amazed at how much I didn't know. One day I was tidying up a kitchen drawer and started to throw out some little balls of string tucked in one corner.

"Oh, don't do that," she said from the nearby table where she sat thumbing through a magazine and ready, at my request, to answer questions.

"I'm just cleaning out the drawer," I replied, defensively.

"That's cotton string. It's hard to get. I save it off the cat food and litter sacks," she replied.

"Yes?" I questioned.

"You need it to sew up stuffed chickens."

So I learned. You save yogurt cups because they hold exactly two servings of rice frozen for future use. You don't ever use a metal spatula or fork within ten feet of a teflon pan. You spread bacon out on a cookie sheet and stick it in the freezer. Then later peel it off and put it in a plastic bag for easy access. You don't add flour to soup after it's hot to thicken it or it will lump. Mix it first with cold milk, then add it. Oh, yes, if there is flour in any soup or sauce, bring it to a boil or it will taste of the flour.

So I was learning and having fun.

So was Elizabeth . . . much of the time.

Sometimes I forgot that what was an expanding experience for me (learning about freezing bacon, for example) was a narrowing experience for her ("I won't be storing bacon anymore"). One Wednesday noon after we finished lunch, Elizabeth asked, "Isn't this the day for a 'control burn' session?"

"Yeah, I guess so," I replied. "Are you 'burning' about something . . . something you want to control?"

"Just a little bit," she said quietly, reflectively. "Well, maybe more than just a little bit. I'm afraid that I haven't really handled my feelings about the kitchen yet."

"Why do you say that?" I asked.

"The cooking and the gardening . . . those are the things I hate most to give up. And when I see you fussing around in the kitchen . . . well, I just about explode sometimes."

"I turn out pretty good food, it seems to me," I said.

"That's not the point. You're a good cook, but . . . "

"But what?"

"That's my space," Elizabeth said despairingly. "I love it. I know you think I'm disorganized, but I know where everything is and why. Like that wooden spoon."

"Wooden spoon?" I asked.

"Yes. That one I keep end up in the Dundee marmalade jar over the stove on the herb shelf. It's the only wooden spoon we have that has any depth. I use it all the time. I keep it right where I can reach. Then you . . ."

"Me, again?"

"Yes, you again, my darling husband and wonderful cook, who I love with everything in me, you . . . you always put it back in the drawer with the other kitchen spoons."

"I'm sorry," I said.

"Don't say you're sorry. That's got nothing to do with it," Elizabeth replied. "I just have to learn to live with that invasion of my space."

"How do we handle that?" I asked. "Or am I asking for solutions again?"

"I guess so," Elizabeth said. "I've just got to learn to live with your way of doing my thing."

"OK," I said. "I'm afraid that's so. But there's so much I don't know. I'm really getting a bang out the stuff you've already taught me. Like freezing the bacon. Instead of staying away when I'm cooking, why don't you stick around and tell me these things one by one . . . in process, as it were?"

"Maybe, sometimes," Elizabeth answered. "But I know that the important thing is for me to blow off like this once in a while."

"If you never blow off more dangerously than that, it's no problem for me," I replied.

"It's all I need," Elizabeth answered. "I feel better already. Let's let it rest for now. I'm OK I need to go lie down for a while."

"Before you go, I have a confession to make," I said, as she gathered up her stuff off the table and started toward the bedroom. "I have promised no more surprise parties. So fair warning. You have a birthday coming up again this week. I still want to make you a birthday cake, try out the sifter and find out how the pop-out pans work. That is a new field for me to conquer."

"Oh my," Elizabeth said with a frayed smile. "I'd better clear out." She got up and kissed me lightly on the cheek and went off to the bedroom.

The surprise party two years earlier had faded into history for everyone but me. I regarded it as a failure that in my fancy catering arrangements for a birthday party I had completely overlooked a cake. I had long since resolved to make one from scratch myself when another birthday rolled around. It felt more honorable to make it from scratch rather than to pour one from a box into the oven.

Now was my chance. So when Elizabeth was well settled in the bedroom, I began this enterprise. I studied an old and trusted cookbook and inched along into the process which moved very slowly for me. I'd read a line and do what it said, then hold things up until I read the next line, often several times. I moved, tentatively, questioningly, from cookbook to bowl to sink, back and forth, with a spoon dripping various ingredients, both powdery and wet, on the counter or, occasionally, on the floor.

I don't know what disturbed Elizabeth, perhaps she came looking for the newspaper, but it seemed to me that she reappeared almost as soon as she had gone to lie down. She came into the kitchen just as I was in the midst of an operation that felt strange to me but I was following the directions in the cookbook precisely.

"What are you doing with all those little bowls?" She had stepped over to the sink to get a drink of water and couldn't pretend that she didn't see the kitchen in a state of confusion.

"What little bowls?" I was stalling.

"Those little sauce dishes."

"Oh, those?" I replied. "I am beating the eggs."

"Beating the eggs?"

"Yes. Beating the eggs! What's wrong with that? Do you bake cakes without eggs? Of course, you use the ready mix," I said with feigned disdain. "I am baking this cake from scratch."

With that I cracked one of the eggs into one of the bowls. I got a bit of shell in it and took a spoon to pick it out and almost pulled all the white out onto the counter.

"Six little bowls?" Elizabeth stood in wonderment. "What *are* you doing, really?"

"I'm getting ready to beat the eggs. The recipe says to beat six eggs separately. It seems funny to me. But I've learned not to ask."

It took Elizabeth forever to stop laughing long enough to explain what was so funny. Even so, I stubbornly argued with her the rest of the day. I still think the writer of that recipe needed some help with the English language.

A few days after this episode Elizabeth commented without a bit of tact on how tight my shirt was across my front. I had eaten most of the cake and much else since spending more time in the kitchen.

"You'd better lose some weight or you'll pull those buttons off. Then that will be another chore for you to learn," she teased good naturedly.

"I don't like myself when I get like this. But it just seems to happen."

"Of course it happens. Just the margarine alone that you put in the scrambled eggs yesterday will swell you up in a month."

"I don't believe it. That little tad of margarine! What would you do? Scramble them in water!"

"I never have, but you could. Simmer down. For heaven's sake. There are some nutritional facts you ought to know if you're going to cook for us. For me, anyway. Like the difference between animal fat and vegetable fat and maybe a few lessons about eggs . . . separated and unseparated!"

CHAPTER 19

As a Sparrow Alone
upon the Housetop

She didn't say anything more about my increasing girth until a few days later when she placed a newspaper clipping by my place at the dinner table. "Now, Mr. Cook," she said, "you can learn about nutrition and lose some weight at the same time."

The clipping was an advertisement in the local paper about a Weight Management course to be offered for local citizens for an extraordinary cut rate by the St. Helena Hospital which specializes in helping people addicted to drugs or tobacco or food. The advertisement claimed that the emphasis was on learning a better way to eat and how to cook for a healthy family. There were to be lectures by physicians and nutritionists and experts in physical exercise.

Elizabeth said she thought this was the sort of thing we should budget for in our renewed determination to be intentional about our marriage in these years. "If you're going to do more of the cooking, I'd like to think you were at least reasonably literate about nutrition."

She was more eager than I about my enrolling for the Weight Management course. This was really strange. She had never seemed to feel that I had a serious weight problem. The course was every Monday night for three months. At first I suspected that she relished the idea of all those quiet Monday evenings by herself. Then I began to see a pattern.

Very gently she was encouraging me to do things by myself. It was a gutsy and generous sacrifice for she really did not like it much when I was away. I suspect she had never fully healed from the trauma which had ensued when, as a young woman, pregnant with her second child and with her four-year-old daughter in hand, she had watched her husband row out into the Sound to do his day's work, never to return, not even his body. So she never had liked to see me go, but now, dependent upon the oxygen machine, worried that she could not turn the little wrench to change the tubing if that became necessary, anxious about power failure— nonetheless, she was bravely pushing me out to try quasi-social events alone. She seldom spoke of what the future held for me. I suspect she thought about it a great deal.

On the appointed Monday evening I made my way alone to St. Helena. The car felt empty, no oxygen tank, no Elizabeth. I found my way into the parking lot of the Seventh Day Adventist Church which had offered the use of their fellowship hall for the Weight Management class. I walked in. There were about twenty women standing around, some of them still at the registration desk, others making uneasy conversation around the edges. There was not another man in sight. My resolve and courage departed, twin deserters under stress. I was glad for an excuse to back out. I could honestly report to Elizabeth that it was obviously a course for women only. I turned right around and out the door before anyone saw me, and started down the sidewalk to the parking lot. I had not gone far when I saw my friend, Lowell Smith, then the mayor of St. Helena, coming up the church walkway.

"You don't need to diet," I said to him as he drew near enough to see who it was speaking to him from the shadows of the church shrubbery.

"I've got ten pounds I want to get off and keep off," he replied. "What are you doing here? You're the one who doesn't need to diet." This was becoming a counter-support group.

"I was just starting home," I said. "I'm not going in there with all those women. I don't think they're expecting any men."

"Courage, brother," Lowell replied. "We'll go together."

So we went in. The women didn't seem to notice us. They just went on with their chatting while Lowell and I and some late-comers signed in and were given the usual big loose-leaf notebook full of duplicated magazine articles, nutrition charts, schedules, recipes and blank pages to record progress.

A tall slender man, perhaps in his early thirties, with a French accent, and a trim older woman with a motherly smile moved toward the head of the tables arranged in a large U-shape in the center of the church hall. The Weight Management class was in session.

Thanks to the Frenchman and the motherly woman, Lowell and I stuck it out to the end of that session and to the end of the course. That is more than could be said for many of the women. Those who did stick it out were a resilient group. Several of them in no way appeared to need the class. I wondered how they saw themselves. Certainly it was an image problem more than a weight problem. That may well have been true of Lowell and me for we were not seriously overweight but we didn't like the way we thought we looked. The women often seemed oblivious to the presence of the two men and with good humor carried on conversation which made me blush.

Often, I felt, the incredible persistent humor covered up a lot of pain and the sadness of the sort which wins scant sympathy from people who easily meet the expectations of *Vogue* magazine or Marlboro country. Society's pressure through ridicule as well as though persistent advertising of weight-loss diets and clubs must help many fat people lose more than weight. They lose joy and self-esteem.

But their humor was often delightfully free. One day they were discussing exercise bikes. A very, very large woman explained that she had wasted her money on one. "Why, honey," she said, "when my knee came up and my breast went down, there was no room for me."

One of the unique features of the program was the opportunity to be weighed submerged in water. In this way the experts were able to get a more accurate picture of body density or the percentage of bone to fat or something. I really have forgotten. But I have not forgotten the evening we all trooped up to the nearby sanitarium swimming pool to get weighed.

It was February or March and the evening was cool. When we got there we were sent to dressing rooms to don the swimming gear we had been instructed to bring with us. So we all got undressed and into the scant coverage of a variety of styles of bathing suits. As the women courageously emerged in twos and threes from their dressing rooms, it became clear that they had a lot more poise than I did walking around half naked. The embarrassment of the flesh does not appear to have a direct correlation to the amount one possesses.

We stood around in the cool night air and wondered when we would get in the water because it was obvious something was delaying the weigh-in. We soon saw the problem; the fabric umbrella over the pool had collapsed. Our instructor, the pleasant, patient, young Frenchman, was lapsing occasionally into agitated French as he directed some workmen who were operating a device to blow the huge bubble up again. It was a very slow process. He finally suggested we go back inside to the warmer exercise room until the pool was ready.

We sat around on the black plastic-covered workout tables or leaned on a weight-lifting machine with our towels around our laps or shoulders and conversed about the cool evening and the deflated pool cover and our curiosity about how we would be weighed. In about 45 minutes, we were summoned for the weigh-in.

The young Frenchman and his helpers had not managed to get the entire plastic bubble up, but at one end of the pool there was enough headroom for us to slip under it and await our turn at the chair in which we would sit to be dunked under the water. For some curious, unanalyzed reason the chair looked to me like the first primitive electric chair. I've always been afraid of water. We were instructed to get all the air out of our lungs and hold it while we were plunged underwater in this chair.

Some of the women could not be squeezed into the chair, so it was proposed that they could be excused. One plucky young woman of exceeding girth said, "No way. I want to be weighed. I can hang onto that chair under the water. Give me a chance." Our fearless, friendly, but weary leader reluctantly allowed her to climb aboard. But, alas, as she and the chair entered the water, she tended to float while the mechanism, a sort of long wooden sea-saw, activated by the trim young Frenchman, pulled the chair down into the water. She tried it a second time with no better result.

I didn't do much better. I got under the water all right but couldn't seem to get the air out of my lungs long enough to meet the requirement. The instructor didn't try very long with me. I was shaking so conspicuously that he feared I would soon have pneumonia. Some of my shaking was not from the chilly night. That large woman, who tended to float too much, and I, were the failures of the weigh-in, and we were both enjoying the notoriety. Everyone was laughing and enjoying one another. Such a strange but wonderful collection of human beings.

On the way home I grew oddly sad. It was different without Elizabeth. She somehow knew that when she insisted I go. Had she been there, we would have enjoyed reviewing the evening all the way home. Here was something we could not ever share in that sense. I tried my best to remember details of the evening and recounted it all to her when I got home. But my words could not make it a shared evening.

During the weeks of the Weight Management class I experimented with some of the recommended recipes at home. One was a vegetarian meat loaf. I didn't make it a second time. In putting it together, with Elizabeth's kibitzing, I learned I had been eating legumes all my life. I felt kin to the fellow who was surprised to learn he had been speaking prose all his life. I did enjoy the milk shake made of a banana and ice and skim milk and a bit of sugar and vanilla. I went heavy on the sugar. By the end of the three months I had lost ten or twelve pounds. And I kept them off for a long time which was really the test of the program. Elizabeth bragged on me and I felt good about myself.

One evening she looked at me as I was carrying some dirty dishes to the kitchen. "Be careful . . . careful," she said, "or you're going to lose them."

"Lose what?" I asked.

"Your pants," she responded. "You're really skinny!"

"You couldn't have said a nicer thing," I replied. "Thank you." I put the dishes down on the counter and went over and kissed her on the cheek. "Remember the last time we saw Aunt Crystal," I continued, "and how she recounted all the things she was glad she didn't have?"

Aunt Crystal was a beautiful person who had had a hard life on a Virginia farm. She spent years rearing her family. (She was careful to explain, quite correctly I believe, that she 'reared' her children and 'raised' her animals and vegetables!) For many many years she also nursed her husband who was a World War I casualty. Our children loved to visit Aunt Crystal on her farm in the summertime because they got to go to the spring and bring back the cool drinking water. They helped feed the pigs and hunted for eggs. The food Aunt Crystal prepared fresh from her garden and hen house was some of the best food any of us ever ate anywhere.

Years later, after the advent of REA and the electricity it brought to her house, and after her talented children prospered and saw the hardness of her life was eased, I saw Aunt Crystal and asked her if she still had her chickens. "No, sir," she answered in her beautifully pitched quiet southern voice, "I don't have any chickens. I don't have any pigs. I don't have a cow. I don't have a wood stove. I can't begin to name the things I am happy to tell you I don't have."

"So," I announced, patting my trimmer front, "I am so happy to tell you how glad I am not to have those pounds." Then turning toward Elizabeth, "And you, my fair lady, what are you glad you don't have?"

"Oh dear," she replied with light-hearted weariness, "I should've known it was coming. You are a perpetual Pollyanna. OK. I suppose I'm glad, most of the time, that I don't have a gloomy husband. But how you keep it up, I don't know."

"What else? Seriously," I pressed.

"Well, sometimes I've thought I should be glad that my stomach still tolerates aspirin. Twelve to fifteen a day, that's a miracle." Then in the fashion of dismissing the subject in favor of something more important, she added, "I don't think of anything else just now. But when you were talking about Aunt Crystal I did think that we ought to take inventory not of what we don't have, but of what we do have."

"Such as?"

"Actually I was thinking how we have complained about all the things we can't do because we are grounded here on this acre. But there are some things we can do because we are grounded here."

"Well, who's Pollyanna now!" I replied. "But like what?" "Like a serious year around vegetable garden. And planting to attract more birds. Things we couldn't keep up with if we were away very much. We can't invite the birds and then go off and leave them," she said.

"OK. And what else?" I pressed.

"You've always claimed you wanted chickens," she said with a mischievous lilt.

"Chickens?"

So it came about that we got chickens. Three chickens! John Mitchell gave us three out of his and Karen's large flock. A red one and a white one and a black one. He claimed that they were not his best and that he thought they were about through laying. They lasted a long time. One of our sons built a small coop and we enjoyed fresh eggs almost all year long. We enjoyed the chickens, too, but not in quite the same way. We never stewed one. We never fried one. We never roasted one. We never ate one in any form. One night a raccoon, though, had quite a fine chicken dinner. The backyard looked like someone had slit open a feather mattress and shaken its contents all over everything and everywhere, the bird bath, the rose bushes, the feeder, the little lemon tree. We were glad we had not named the chickens. We did not get any more. My cholesterol was rising.

Long before that unhappy event, the useful pleasure we had had with the chickens caused us to think about what else we could do and enjoy because we were at home twelve months a year. We were having a conversation on that subject, brainstorming ideas, when Elizabeth asked me one day if I had lost interest in becoming a monk.

CHAPTER 20

Creeping Things and Flying Fowl

Whenever Elizabeth and I discussed various options before us as we resolved to make this short ride together as pleasant as possible, you may be sure one of those options was not that I should become a monk! It soon developed that what she was remembering now, in her question about my becoming a monk, was my tremendous admiration for an ecumenical Christian community in San Francisco, now affiliated with the Orthodox Church. I had long envied this religious order which displays a spontaneous joy in life while they work together operating Raphael House. It is reputedly the only emergency shelter in San Francisco which admits whole families. A feature writer for the *San Francisco Examiner* explained, "Raphael House . . . offers families who live there an environment that is warm, peaceful and simple. (They) receive mounds of spiritual and community support so they can get their lives back on track." (Bradley Inman, March 24, 1991.)

The sisters and brothers who are members of this order and live permanently in this community are both married and single, but they are all under solemn vows of poverty, chastity, obedience, service and humility. Few visitors can remain unmoved by a visit to Raphael House. The spirit of realistic, relaxed caring is contagious, caring not only for one another, but for the defeated and broken parents and children who make it to their door. I had often told Elizabeth how much I envied their life and how deeply

128

satisfying it must be. So now I wondered what she had in mind when she asked me, mostly in jest, what had happened to my desire to take the vows and join up with the sisters and brothers of Raphael House.

"Are you encouraging me to become a celibate?" I asked.

"Be serious, please," she ordered in friendly fashion. "Besides, they aren't celibates at Raphael House. Their vow is chastity."

"What brought all this up, anyway?" I asked.

"I've been thinking," Elizabeth responded earnestly. "You know what? We are essentially parasites! I think that's what bothers me the most these days. At least I am. No good to anybody about anything that really matters!"

"What do you mean?" I asked.

"Doesn't it worry you?" she answered, looking at me, her great brown eyes filled with painful questioning. "We're living a completely self-centered life. Back and forth between wonderful friends and a wonderful doctor and a beautiful garden! But it's all for us. I don't contribute a thing, except I still vote. Little good that does."

"You give to a lot of good causes," I reminded her. "More than I think you should, sometimes. Everything from wildlife to AIDS."

"Little enough," she said, "considering the relative luxury in which we live. But worse, really. Sometimes I feel that we live as though no one else in the whole world was hurting!"

"We sure are on the receiving end of things," I said.

"But when you're sick, it's just awful," she whispered.

"What's just awful?" I asked.

"You get . . . you get so you expect it. That's a worse sickness than the sickness." She spoke reflectively as though she were speaking only to herself. As I looked at this little woman, her back now so twisted with arthritis that she couldn't get a skirt to hang straight and her face strung up with plastic tubes, I said quietly, "You forget what you do for everyone who comes here. You just won't give yourself any credit."

Elizabeth was not hearing any compliments or anything else. She had the unmistakable look of someone giving birth to an idea. "I think there is more we can do than just sit here," she said with awakened alertness. "I had an idea today when you and Amador were working in the garden."

"On with it. What do you propose?"

She looked straight at me with just the hint of mischief in her face. "I propose," she said quietly, "that we give the garden to Raphael House. You can be a monk right here . . . a monk with a hoe. Maybe a bird will land on your shoulder."

Before I could say a word, Elizabeth hurried on, with her eyes shining brightly and her face so alight that the plastic tubing itself glistened. "You and I will give the garden to Raphael House," she announced gaily. "We can plan it together. I can order the seeds and supervise. I'll use money from the back of the checkbook. You and Amador can do the work, the other work. Is the truck in good enough shape to drive into San Francisco?"

So it was that the Holy Gleaning Co., Unlimited was born. Elizabeth was president, vice president, and treasurer. I held all the other offices including fertilizer chairperson and truck driver. The first year we found we couldn't begin to grow enough ourselves to make the bi-weekly trips worthwhile. So the next year we got friends in the church and neighbors involved. One of the members of the church, until then unknown to me, makes his living as a "purveyor of fine foods." He joined in the effort. Anything that was not super-special could not go to the exclusive and pricey restaurants and grocers he supplied so, after our project was underway, sometimes Raphael House got quail and frog legs and edible flowers.

All kinds and conditions of human beings now participate in the Holy Gleaning Co., the local grocer, two or three rich people with large "kitchen gardens," older people with only a small patch of earth to cultivate, hunters with too much venison in the freezer or a guilty conscience, vineyardists who have some table grapes, organic gardeners making a statement, and commercial gardeners making a living. Raphael House finds use for everything, even unlimited zucchini!

Elizabeth revelled in its success. I suspect she was also pleased that she had arranged a chore which took me to San Francisco regularly. I usually made the trips by myself and appreciated the time with my own thoughts. She knew that one common problem of caregivers is the difficulty they encounter in arranging for a change once in a while, a bit of time off to recharge without feeling guilty. One of the most thoughtful gifts we received from members of our "little family of the heart" was their time, moving in for a few hours or even a few days to afford us both a change.

This broadened and useful purpose for all the vegetables and fruits we could grow gave us both immense satisfaction, but Elizabeth especially. She missed the gardening more sorely than the cooking. Her arthritis had limited her work in the soil even before we retired and she was never reconciled to that limitation. Although she could no longer get up to her elbows in the soil, she could get in the soil up to *my* elbows!

Ever since we first bought this country place my role had clearly been that of the hired man so far as all the growing things were concerned, plants and animals, indoors and out. Elizabeth was the boss and in these years of confinement she could boss almost as well from indoors as outdoors! Where she ever learned all about soil and seeds, cucumber beetles and poison oak, remains a mystery. She really was incredibly knowledgeable even to the Latin names. Amador, who had come to be like a third son, would say to me when we were working together, about some agricultural question, "We'd better ask the lady." She taught me (and Amador, too!), for example, with expressive language not often heard in our house, not to prune the quince bushes before they have bloomed no matter how much their ragged look offends my neat and tidy inclinations. "Tidy up your dresser drawers," she said, "if you must tidy something."

This "tidy" business was always a source of conflict. It came to a head one day in an argument about landscaping. I wanted to cultivate a broad smooth green lawn in our backyard. I fantasized it to be so well manicured that we could refer to it as "the garden" (as in Buckingham, not as in vegetable). I have had "backyards" all my life and before I die I wanted a "garden" with grass like a putting green and squared off rosebeds lined with sweet alyssum. We postponed the "discussion" to the next "control burn" session and forestalled an immediate conflagration. At the "control burn" hour I explained all this to Elizabeth who listened patiently but I sensed I wasn't making much progress.

"Why are you so opposed to any semblance of order?" I asked with a bit of sarcasm in my voice and a vision of her desktop in my mind.

"It's for the birds," she answered.

"You mean 'order' is for the birds?"

"No. I mean 'disorder' is for the birds."

"Don't put me down."

"I'm not putting you down."

"Well, then don't say that what I like is for the birds. No, that's not what you said, you . . . "

"What you like isn't for the birds." We both began to laugh. Elizabeth persisted. "That's the problem. What I want is for the birds, real birds, the phoebes and the toebees and the white-crowned sparrows. Where are they going to hide in your neat manicured garden? The ground birds need the weeds."

I began to understand. Eventually we worked out a compromise. We moved the flower beds in fifteen feet or so from the back fence between our yard and the vineyard which surrounds our property except on the highway side. Between the house and the relocated flowerbeds I was allowed to manicure as much lawn as I wanted. But between the flowerbeds and the fence was nature's own, left in the rough for the birds. Little low weeds still flourish there without a hoe to disturb them or a spray of chemicals to wipe them out. And the lizards slip in and out and between the California poppies which have moved in to that unsophisticated environment. In that reserve one tremendously overgrown and prickly pyracantha never feels the pruning shears and I must admit it seems full of birds all year round. The roses and the smooth green lawn are doing nicely, too, in their part of "the garden"!

In some ways the role of hired man was easier for me when Elizabeth became subject to her fifty foot tether. Once in a while, in sheer desperation to feel the soil and see the first corn sprouting or check up on me and end her loneliness, Elizabeth would pull out the tubing and surprise me at the garden gate. She would last a moment or two and then we would go back into the house together and play a game of cards. But most of the time she supervised my gardening "in absentia." I would catch myself looking over my shoulder to be sure she hadn't escaped the house when I was getting ready to do some rash thing like pulling up a sickly tomato plant. If it had the slightest sign of life in it, she would keep me nursing it along for weeks. My attitude was more pragmatic: "Shape up, little plant, or ship out." The weeding went faster and was easier for me when she was housebound.

Maybe it was easier for her as well, not watching me too closely. Many a time I heard a sickening gasp when she saw me "weed" out some growing thing which was out of line or appeared clearly unenthusiastic about being in my care. She thought of plants as though they were really living things, like animals. Before I knew much about composting and the care of the soil I thought she was even digging graves for dead plants when she worked them down into the slumbering autumn earth.

One day she left a comic strip on my desk without comment. It pictured a pre-teen girl watering and nurturing a single little flower, a daisy or aster of some sort. In the next frame her brother comes riding through on his bike in a cloud of dust and dog. She screams at him, "Michael! Come back here. You just ran over a flower."

"So? Look around! There's millions of them! So I ran over a stupid flower! Why should you care?"

Looking down sadly at the crushed little flower she replies, "I knew this one." (*For Better or For Worse* by Lynn Johnson, SR Press Democrat, Sunday, May 29, 1988.)

I hope that child's name is Elizabeth.

* * * * * * * *

Elizabeth did allow me, in one sense, to be a specialist, a fertilizer specialist. Not all fertilizers. I specialized in chicken fertilizer, that is, chicken manure. Really, chicken shit! You can tell people's degree of involvement with this fertilizer by what they call it. "Shit" is not a very pretty word, but then chicken fertilizer is not especially pleasant stuff. I really never was comfortable to hear Elizabeth refer casually to chicken "shit." "Can't you please say 'manure'?" I would ask her in a Victorian frenzy of genteelism. I'm still baffled that she could say that word at all. We were both reared by parents who were very particular about language. We were discouraged from saying even such mild words as "gosh" or "heck." "Might as well come right out and say 'God' and 'hell'," my father once explained.

A neighbor of ours raises chickens, lots of them, thousands of them. They come and go in cycles and in between he sells off truckloads of the manure, the shit. It's mixed with rice husks, I believe, or whatever it is on the floor of the coops. When the coops are cleaned, the stuff is piled up out in the middle of his farmyard. It's a big pile. Big. Not like a bread box or a telephone booth, but big like a barn with a good sized loft! Not only is the pile tremendously large, but the mixture itself is tremendously strong, raw stuff. Don't ever try to mulch with it. I did once and just about finished off a nice little kitchen garden Elizabeth had established. Our vastly expanded garden for Raphael House used lots of our neighbor's chickens' by-product.

This mixture is not only strong and raw, but also, as you can well guess, it smells to high heaven. But as you may not guess, it not only smells to high heaven, but once released it tends actually to float toward heaven. You just can't hold it down. When you pitch a shovel full on to your truck, a cloud of strong, raw, stinking dust rises up. Hardy young men wear masks when they move it anywhere as well as always checking out the wind before deciding which side of the pile to tackle. One day I went over to my neighbor when the pile was high and he gave me all I could load by hand into my prized old pickup. The truck has a camper shell on it or he would have loaded it for me with his machine.

It was almost noon when I finished the load. Actually I didn't "finish." The truck wasn't "finished" as in being "full." But I was "finished" as in being "done in," so I decided to go through town and pick up a couple of hamburgers for Elizabeth and me to have for lunch. I parked in the space provided for customers at the drive-in and stepped up to the window and placed my order. Then I returned to the truck to wait for my number to be called.

I soon realized that there were two attractive women eating their lunch in the car parked next to my truck. I didn't recognize them but it was obvious they knew me or thought they did and wanted to talk. I was flattered and pleased by the prospect. So I clambered down out of the truck and tried to look my affable best as I sauntered over to their car. So what if they were mistaken and didn't know me? I wondered why they didn't roll down the window if they wanted to speak to me. It is really annoying to me when people try to have a conversation with you but won't do the simplest thing in order to be heard like taking their hands out of their mouths or, in this case, rolling down the car window.

I couldn't quite hear what they said and didn't want to press up to the window as if I were hard of hearing or trying to be fresh. They were such well-groomed women that I wasn't prepared to hear for quite a while what they were saying. I guess my puzzled expression said to them, "I beg your pardon," or something like that. Finally, one of them cracked her window just a trifle but quite enough for me to hear her clearly, "For God's sake, get that shit out of here. We're eating."

I waited for my hamburgers up by the window after moving my truck out into the street. I understood.

I had another experience with fertilizer and communication which I simply did not understand until Elizabeth explained it to me where no one could possibly overhear us. It happened one day when the county farm agent was trying to help us take better care of our fruit trees. Among a lot of other good counsel he instructed me about fertilizing the apple trees. "Put a coffee can full of chicken manure under each tree," he said.

"Do I put holes in the can?" I asked him.

"What for?"

"To get the fertilizer out of the can into the soil."

The agent looked at Elizabeth and didn't say a word. The rest of the time he was there, I felt he was talking more with her than with me, almost as though I weren't there.

That's pretty much how it has been through the years. So this was not a role reversal I welcomed in anyway. I really felt inadequate except as the laborer. The garden even more than the kitchen was Elizabeth's territory. Whenever I did any work in the garden, she was always there, a sort of instant *Better Homes and Gardens* reference book. When I took over the garden and discovered I had to make an unilateral decision, I was very insecure. When the lettuce I brought in was tough or the artichokes were full of earwigs, I was sure I had made some mistake. Occasionally, however, there were such massive problems to be solved that I ran to the house at once for consultation, such as the morning I went out to hoe and water and found a very large deer lying dead with a broken neck in the zucchini.

I wasn't a bit concerned about losing a few zucchini. Nature, as an agent of God, also works in mysterious ways. Anything to get rid of a few zucchinis. But I was worried about the deer. What was I going to do with it! I rushed to the house for a consultation.

"Guess what's in the garden?"

"What?"

"A deer. A dead deer."

"How did he get in?"

"He must have jumped the garden fence. I think I may have left the driveway gate open last night."

We have a deer fence around our acre and aim to keep the driveway gate closed during deer season or they will come in and feast on the camellias and roses. Then we have a lower rabbit proof fence around the vegetable garden. It was this lower fence with the always closed gate which the deer had obviously hurdled.

"I think he must have caught his front foot on the fence as he went over and fallen on his head. Anyway, I am sure his neck is broken."

"Oh, the poor thing."

"What about me?"

"What about you?"

"What the devil am I going to do with the carcass?"

"Why bury it, of course."

"Bury it?"

"You must make some good out of it. It will be good for the soil."

"That's easy enough for you to say. You should see it. It's enormous."

"You could do it in the time we're arguing about it."

So I returned reluctantly to the garden after getting our stoutest spade from the shed. I surveyed the territory and decided that the only place for a grave was in one corner where the compost pile had been in the Spring and where I had not yet planted anything. I measured the deer with the handle of the shovel and then marked off a grave.

I started digging. Very soon I realized that it would have to be a pretty big grave if I buried it on its side. Why not bury it legs up. Then the grave would not have to be so wide. I returned to the deer with the shovel and measured the legs. I returned to the grave site and began digging a narrower pit. Very soon I realized that the grave might be narrow if I buried it legs up, but it would have to be very deep and probably I would end up with either a crippled back or four deer legs sticking up out of the ground where the compost pile had been. I had the macabre thought that I could chop off the protruding legs, possible with the heavy duty lawn mower. Somehow I didn't think that would be acceptable. Besides, what would I tell Bob Mitrovich, who serviced the mower and regarded me dubiously as a farmer.

I didn't return to the house for further advice. I knew Elizabeth would be sympathetic. But I also feared she would be very firm about going ahead with the grave. What else could I do. Then . . . then, it hit me with a great liberating flash. The State Highway Department! Their crews remove the carcasses of the deer killed along the thoroughfares of the state. We live on a state highway. If I could get that deer out to the highway and dump it surreptitiously, eventually the Highway Department would pick it up. Why I could even call in and report a dead deer in the road in front of our house.

The problem now was how to move the body out to the road and dump it without being apprehended by either Elizabeth or other authorities. Our older son had given us a Vermont garden cart. It is a strong and versatile contraption with large bicycle wheels making it possible to pull great loads of firewood or heavy compost or gravel. I ran for the shed to get the cart, moving like one possessed by a great idea.

I brought the cart to the deer but found the deer heavy and in an awkward position to lift into the cart. But this marvelous cart is not easily intimidated. The front end can be tipped forward so the front side is parallel to the ground. Then you push stuff on and tip the cart back upright. That is exactly what I did with the deer. The remaining problem was the deer's eyes. Its head was twisted back on the cart at a strange angle due to the fractured neck. And the eyes were open! They focussed directly on anyone who pushed that cart. I thought I heard the spirit of the deer admonishing me, "You'd better not let Elizabeth see this little procession."

We got safely past the house, down the driveway, and out into the highway. I decided that I didn't want to dump it very near our property. Who knows? It may be weeks before the maintenance crew finds this carcass which will soon be competing with the chicken fertilizer for our nostrils' attention. So I was pushing on down the road a few yards with the deer's head bent crazily upwards and its eyes fixed on me when I heard a car coming down the highway to my rear just beyond the curve past our driveway.

There was no time to hide and no place to hide, but providentially there were several beat up beer cans and other trash beside the road. Immediately I busied myself being the good citizen, out cleaning up the public domain and bending over my cart in such a way as to conceal, as much as I could, its load and my unlawful intent.

When I straightened up from this belabored good citizenship I realized the passing car was slowing down and stopping and backing up toward me and that it had the unmistakable smell about it of the California Highway Patrol. The officer got out and came toward me. I was born with a guilty conscience and I could feel my heart pressing for passage around my soft palate.

"You're being a good citizen I see," said a middle-aged uniformed officer with a paunch doubtless made generous by years of patrolling the California highways. The uniforms always seem so incongruous to me on such well-settled men.

"Yep," I said, reaching down at the same time for a dirty Pepsi bottle I had just spied half buried in the rocks and gravel of the roadside.

"I see you have a deer, too."

"Yep."

"Pretty big one."

"Yep. I think his neck got broken." I had regained my nouns and verbs.

"It's good of you to move it out of the highway," the officer said. "They're as much a traffic hazard dead as alive. Here. Let me help you put it off on the shoulder of the highway."

"Why, thank you, officer."

"I'll notify the maintenance crew," he said. "They'll pick it up in a couple of hours I imagine."

"Why, thank you, sir."

"Lots of trash along the highways these days," he observed as he turned a bit to look up and down the road for more litter.

"Lots," I agreed.

"Good of folks like you to help pick it up."

"Oh, that's nothing."

"You know," said the officer. "I have seen people dump their household trash right on the side of the road."

"You have?" I echoed.

"Illegal, too," the paunchy officer said as he turned and squeezed back into his patrol car. "Well, thanks and take care." And he was off.

When I came back to the house Elizabeth asked about the deer.

"It's taken care of," I assured her.

"Thank you, dear. I know it was an awful chore."

"Not as bad as I feared," I said.

CHAPTER 21

The Heights of the Mountains
Are His Also

Our house was a small redwood farmhouse when we discovered it and claimed it in 1964. It had one tremendous room with a brick fireplace and a ceiling framed by the lines of the roof. There was a tiny bedroom and a kitchen and bath, but the house was mostly that one generous room. It was the perfect retreat for us during those busy crowded years of active professional life. We always felt cheated if we did not get twenty-four hours under its roof or in its garden every week. It was large enough to welcome crowds but on rainy days when the fire was built it closed itself down gently around us, protectively, as we lost ourselves in Ellery Queen or the Sunday magazine sections accumulated over several weeks.

The tiny bedroom was big enough for a bed which is the most generous thing one could say for it; and the bathtub did hold water and the toilet did flush, ordinarily. When we went to bed, climbing over the foot of the bed to get to the inside side, or after a warm bath, pulling ourselves up, wet and cold, out of the handleless tub, we dreamed of the day we would have a master bedroom and a modern bath. When that dream came true, then this skimpy room and antiquated bath would do nicely for guests!

We sketched and measured and discussed and argued about what that new room would be like—a light in the closet, space for Elizabeth's desk and her tattered copies of *Western Gardening* and the *Audubon Guides to North American Birds and Wildflow-*

ers. There would be a shelf near the window for the binoculars always at the ready, and maybe we could add a little deck with absolute privacy, and surely a shower! Many years later with the help of a modest inheritance and the skill and patience of Paul Kelley, A.I.A., who took his fees in weekend visits, that new room (really a wing, including a modern kitchen) finally came into being.

Always there was one feature in our dreams that was never questioned. Our bedroom must have a great window facing Mt. St. Helena, exposing us boldly to the vast privacy we had on that side of our single acre. Nothing but cattle, and later vineyards, stood between us and the fire lookout tower on Mt. St. Helena. That dominating mountain rises virtually from sea level at our garden gate to almost five thousand feet. To this day the fire lookout atop the mountain remains for us aloof and unknown. It is a distant vague squarish structure distinguishable only with field glasses. But at night during the fire season it becomes a tiny diamond of light, telling us it will keep an eye on things while we sleep.

The mountain had kept guard over us now, twelve months a year for the past six difficult years. How often, I wondered, during that hot summer of '89 with its endless nights, did Elizabeth watch that tiny light. She would lie quietly awake with her heart working so hard that sometimes I could see her small frame shaking to contain it although she appeared oblivious to the ruckus it made. Sometimes I thought that even if her heart did not burst, mine surely would. Occasionally I would break the silence of our sleeplessness. I thought if she spoke, she might shift her body someway and ease the pounding in her fragile chest.

"Can you see the fire lookout from your side of the bed?" I asked her one night when we were just settling down.

"Oh, yes," she said. "I wonder if that man up there is awake, too. How does it work, anyway?"

"For one thing," I replied, "it's not a man up there. It's a woman. Or so Chick told me the other day."

"A woman! Good for her! What do you suppose her schedule is? She has to sleep sometime. Do you suppose she sets her alarm and gets up every hour and takes a look around?"

"I have no idea. But it's a happy thought . . . for us if not for her."

"At least when I see the light, I know the mountain is still there."

At that simple moment in our time together I lifted a silent doxology to whatever angels stood guard over our marriage, grateful in a way I am glad I had never anticipated I would be, grateful that we had not given up on our resolve about the picture window when we finally built the "master suite."

Elizabeth didn't worship the mountain, of course. Or did she, maybe, in a sense. One day she quoted the familiar lines about the hills, endlessly used in inspirational talks for young people in mountain camps, "I will lift up mine eyes unto the hills, from whence cometh my help."

"Don't push that too far," I said. "You know what the Psalmist meant. The enemy was in the hills. Getting ready to attack. The poet was explaining that his help was not in the hills but in the Lord. I think some scholars translate it, 'I will lift up mine eyes unto the hills. Period! From whence cometh my help. Question mark.' I think that's nearer the original intent. It's not a proof text for nature worship."

"So what?" she replied with some heat. "Now who is taking the Bible literally instead of seriously?" That was a charge I frequently made about people who spoil the Bible with literalism. "I haven't got any enemies up in that mountain unless it is some fool hunter with a gun out of season . . . not even the rattlesnakes."

"Well said. You're quite right." I replied, struggling to cover my tracks. After all, this wasn't a class in exegesis.

She had been looking toward the mountain while she talked. She fell silent for a moment and I thought her eyes were fixed on the light in the fire tower. Then she turned to me and continued very privately, her voice restrained but urgent, the tone that always emerged when she felt it was her loving duty to persuade me that a sermon I was proposing would surely bomb.

"Sometimes I wonder if all your 'study' of the Bible is a substitute for hearing it. What about Horeb and Sinai and the Mount of Transfiguration! I heard something about them in the Baptist Sunday School. What do you call it, 'the transcendence of God,' God's glory? Something like that echoes in me when I reach out to the mountain. But that mountain is more than just a symbol to me."

She grew quiet. Her annoyance with me was only momentary. She was trying to express something important and beautiful to her. Something she felt I was missing. She gazed at the mountain and mused, almost as if I were not there, "I don't think that the mountain is God."

"I know that, Liz," I said in the silence between us.

"But it's wonderful to look at it," she continued, "and at all the rest of this incredible creation and wonder if it all is not in some sense the body of God. All of it!—the soil our hands caress . . . and the most remote vision our astro-physic eye can scan."

"'Astro-physic eye?' Now who is giving a lecture?" I teased.

She smiled momentarily and then shot right back, "Well then don't you lecture me about the 'original intent' of the 121st Psalm. Right now I could care less what the 'original intent' was. I know what it *intends* for me. Everyday I 'lift up my eyes' to that mountain. I'm so glad . . . glad not only to be part of such an incredible creation, but an observer, too. Somehow that feels more than being part of it. Maybe that is how we are like God. You are more responsible . . . or responsible in a different way. It's sort of the difference between loving yourself and loving your neighbor. Or maybe more the difference between loving some object you nail together, something you make, however beautiful, and loving something that has its own being. Something alive."

She went on as though she had just got this all figured out and had to finish it up before it slipped away, "*You* can chop down a tree without even noticing the live sap. I just can't understand that. You have no idea how glad I really was when my hands got so bad I couldn't manage the gun anymore so you wouldn't ask me to shoot any more rattlesnakes."

She smiled wryly with that confession, and turned back toward the mountain. After a time she spoke very quietly. It was almost as though she were speaking only to herself. "Other people have music and art and poetry. I have the mountain and the earth and the quince bush and the brown towhee."

I moved toward her. She seldom expressed herself with such feeling except when the evening news showed oil slick covering wetlands or some politician making flimsy excuses for not funding school lunches in West Oakland. I put my arms around her.

We shifted in the bed. I kicked the sheet off my feet altogether. It was still hot. Elizabeth turned toward me and laid her head low on my chest. It was quiet in the room and we were quiet.

Finally Elizabeth spoke. So softly I could scarcely hear her. "You hardly ever hug me anymore," she said.

It was love's long suppressed rebuke . . . offered carefully. It silenced any easy response with the pain of its delivery. Finally I replied, "It's the tubing, I guess. I feel like I will shut off your air or hurt your nostrils."

"Let me worry about that. Trust me. And your Dr. Levy. Just hold me. Hold on tight."

And I did.

After a long time, just resting in each other, she pushed back gently and looked up at me. "As long as I have you and the mountain, I'll be all right."

I pulled her toward me until the warmth of her breasts touched me. Then slowly, deliberately, deeply, we kissed, tubing and all.

* * * * * * * *

Except for the heroic window, our bedroom is a modest affair tucked in behind the kitchen. First-time visitors pause involuntarily when they step into it, surprised by the window. It takes their eyes from the perpetually disorganized order on Elizabeth's desk and from the family snapshots stuck in the edge of every mirror and picture frame in the room and from the treasured knicknacks Elizabeth lined up on the long windowsill even when *she* was doing the dusting!—a slender oval of solid glass with a minuscule dogwood in full bloom frozen in its crystal center; a smooth green jade turtle her mother, a painstaking and untiring shopper, bought for her one Christmas by mail when the aging lady finally had to let her fingers do her walking for her; a perfectly formed pine cone from the immense conifer which shades our driveway, a much too splendid specimen, Elizabeth protested, even to use to light the grate fire; three glass bluebirds blown to life in graduated sizes by some Kentucky craftsman; a ceramic mushroom; a spider with a sassy stance sculptured out of barbed wire.

But the great window steals the show. It is six feet wide and almost twice that high as it pushes itself up grandly to touch the highest point where the peaked roof of the house and the ceiling of the room are one. I suspect that sometimes the visitor who is brought up short by this window and its spectacular view may actually be gasping at the thought of washing it. Spiders are active enough that within 24 hours of any effort to shine it up and bring down the webs, there are more, so cleaning the window could easily worry any visiting housekeeper. But there are two other problems with the window.

The first concerns the view, not from the house but into the house! At intervals during the growing season, the vineyard, which is our immense backyard, although beyond our fence and beyond our control, is dusted by an expert and daring pilot in a very low-flying helicopter. If there is little or no wind and the time is appropriate, we are awakened at dawn three or four times each summer, by a 'copter zooming at our house.

On occasion we have had guests asleep when the attack on the vineyard begins. It feels as though some pilot is in desperate trouble, bringing his plane down full throttle, directly at our roof. On one such morning when my sister, Irene, a frequent and helpful visitor, was here, she knocked at our bedroom door without so much as a robe over her flimsy pajamas. It was the first time she had experienced the attack.

"What should we do?" she asked. "I thought maybe I should go outside in case the house fell in. It sure was shaking."

We laughed and took her in for the duration. She sat down on the edge of our bed, I pulled up on one elbow, Elizabeth turned toward the window, and together we watched the sorties by the pilot and the clouds of sulphur he left swirling over the vines in his wake. "You know," I said to my sister and my wife, "I bet that man can see us lounging on this bed."

I really didn't think so, but if we could see him, and we could, plainly, there in his plastic bubble, legs and all, why couldn't he see us?

"Well," Elizabeth said, "why don't you wave to him the next time he comes by?"

So I did. I got out of bed, which may have been cheating a bit for this experiment, and stood beside it. The next time he came by I waved. There was no response. But then when he reached the end of that swoop just beyond the distant high vineyard fence, he turned back more sharply than usual, I thought, to make his next attack on the vines. As he did so, he came down so low that the water in the birdbath in the middle of our backyard trembled. And he waved!

"Look," I shouted over the din, "he waved. He can see us!"

"Oh, no, I hope not," said my sister fingering her scant and thin summer pajamas.

Elizabeth laughed. "Wait until he tells the neighbors that the preacher has two women in his bed." I sat down beside her on the bed. And I laughed. And Irene laughed until she had to go find a piece of Kleenex.

We have never met this pilot, but the next time we were attacked when Irene was visiting, she was ready with her camera and got a dramatic snapshot of him in his flying bubble. I sent the picture to him through Herb Westfall, the ranch manager, our neighbor. I hope the pilot stuck it up somewhere in his cockpit.

The other problem the great window presents does not lend itself to snapshots and does not amuse us. In the first summer of her illness Elizabeth found each added degree of temperature an added weight upon her breathing. The window, her great consolation, was fast becoming her great curse. That splendid window, bringing the mountain to her, also unmercifully magnified the summer heat. It faces northeast and most of the year the sun touches it gently or not at all. But when May begins yearning for June, the sun refuses to rest in the south and pushes its way around the house to sear that northeast window and bake this favorite room.

"We should not complain," Elizabeth said one day, looking out across the green vineyard as we prepared to abandon the room for the rest of the day. "What do you think your tomatoes would look like if we had lovely cool summers!"

"And the wine? Hot by day. Cool by night. The grapes wouldn't be any better than Fresno's."

We laughed at each other.

"We could hire out to the Chamber of Commerce. But truth will out," I said. "It's damn hot and you know it. This room is impossible in July."

"But think what it would be if it didn't cool off at night. I actually turned on the electric blanket one night last week."

So the annual visit of the sun is welcomed in our valley by the plants and seeds and those who nourish them, and loudly applauded by those with their money in the vineyards, but studiously ignored in the Tourist Bureau propaganda. The sun pounded on our favorite room like a mortal enemy until it got as hot as a pyrex baking dish and cooked the contents including us. I was worried sick about this summer. It was only June but the temperature was soaring. Moving out of the room every afternoon was becoming increasingly difficult for Elizabeth . . . and me.

"It's only hot for a few hours for a few weeks, and then only a few hours a day," we claimed to a friend sweltering with us one day as the thermometer pushed up to 99. "When it gets really bad we take a couple of lounge chairs out under the oak tree and turn on a lawn sprinkler."

"May I fetch you a lounge chair or two? or three?" our friend asked soberly. "Or do we have to hit 100° first?"

Indeed, that is how we had managed for many summers. But now it was different and before the first summer of Elizabeth's illness had passed into history, we succumbed to an air conditioner for the room with the great window. But even if we turned it on early in the morning, it was no match for the heat pouring in through the glass. And Elizabeth's frugality made it almost impossible for her to turn it on before the room was really hot.

If we turn it on early in the morning, it makes the room habitable, but barely. So as this terribly hot summer of '89 descended upon us and Elizabeth found heat more and more intolerable and moving out of the room every afternoon more and more difficult, we had to face the question of covering the window. Elizabeth was caught. She did not want to give up the view, even for a few weeks. But the heat was her enemy. It made it difficult for her to speak. When she came to the table to eat, as she always did, she would have to sit and rest a few minutes before facing food or conversation.

She kept a glass of water filled with ice nearby all the time. It was part of her equipment. She moved from room to room guiding the trailing oxygen tube around the corners and through the doors behind her with the hand that was not much good to her, while she carried the ice water with the other, hanging on to it more fiercely than she did the tube. Sometimes the tube would get hung up under the refrigerator or some other hazard along the way and jerk her to a stop. Occasionally for this reason or another, she would lose her grip on the glass sending ice cubes skittering over the floor. Reaching a chair, she would contemplate the mess and wait for her breath to return. Seldom did she say anything. Once she explained to me that by the time she got enough breath to cuss, the need had passed. Another frustration!

John Mitchell stopped by one morning early in the summer of '89 to bring us some fresh bread from Karen's bakery. At least that is the excuse he gave for the visit but it was easily 18 miles out of his way. Quite a trip just to deliver bread, special as it was. I suspect he wanted to see how we were faring with the heat. It was John who had insisted that we get an air conditioner the first summer that Elizabeth had had to go public with her illness or else hide the oxygen tank.

John had been very troubled when he realized how seriously ill she must be. After that he even more frequently turned his Toyota pickup in at our driveway and pretended to test once again with pride the bridge he had built for us. His first bridge and so far as I know his only bridge.

"My nephew has bought a new 18 wheeler," I teased him one day. "I expect him to come visiting any day now."

"God," John replied with a wounded look, "you wouldn't really?"

Usually by the time we had responded to the sound of his tires in the gravel, our front door would be filled with his impressive blonde hunkiness. He was worried about our problem with the heat. He knew the air conditioner was inadequate for that room with all that glass and the high ceiling. Perhaps he felt some responsibility for not persuading us to install central heat and air conditioning when we built the new wing. That was an extravagance and luxury we wouldn't even contemplate. At least Elizabeth wouldn't! You would think she had gone hungry during the Depression. John had warned us when the house was built that the window would be a summer liability. Now he was alarmed.

On this morning which promised a very hot day, he not only brought us bread but he had in his truck a redwood lattice screen he had devised for the highest part of the window. He had brought his long ladder and Elizabeth and I watched from inside as he installed it. It fit perfectly because he had come by some other time and measured perfectly. It fit the upper reaches of the window very well, but that really did not help much. But it did provide a structure from which we could hang some kind of curtain.

I had long been convinced that we would have to take more radical action even if it meant the sacrifice of the view. Better do what I had long dreaded now while there was some help. When I saw John's long ladder still at the window, I was spurred to act.

I left Mitchell and Elizabeth speculating about other solutions and went to the shed and came back with a roll of the black degradable plastic we use for mulch in the vegetable garden. Standing at the window, John looked first at it and then at me with disdain as though to say with irritation, "Oh you and your solutions!" I ignored his accusation. It was obvious that *his* solution wasn't going to work. I motioned him outside and without a word moved the ladder back into place. With his reluctant cooperation and the help of a large stapler, I hung the black plastic from his lattice work. Then we went inside to measure the effect.

"How is that, Elizabeth?" I asked blithely as we stood there in the semi-darkness at mid morning.

"It cuts the sun all right," she said.

"It also cuts the view," I added. "Can you live with that?"

"Of course," she said. "The mountain will still be there when the sun has gone south again."

Mitchell and I looked at each other. He didn't say much except that he was late for an appointment on up the valley. I walked out to his truck with him.

"That damn black plastic is for the birds," he said. "Shit."

"It's better than the sun," I countered.

"I'm not so sure," John replied. And with that he was gone.

The next morning he was back. I went to the front door to meet him. "Elizabeth sleeping?" he asked.

"No. We are sitting in front of the air conditioner and playing cards . . . with the light on! Come on in."

"I've got something in the truck. I'll get it."

I went back to the bedroom and reported to Elizabeth that it was Mitchell at the door. I had scarcely told her who was there when we saw and heard the black plastic, covering the window, shake and rip like an angry racoon was climbing up it. As it split in several places, we saw Mitchell, who had come around the side of the house, pulling it down, tearing it off the window as though it were diseased and needed to be quickly banned from the premises.

With the plastic on the ground at his feet, Mitchell looked into the room and motioned for me to come help him. He didn't say a word until he had his long ladder in place and began wrestling with a roll of white fabric.

"I think maybe we've got something here," he said.

His large hands, hardened with callouses yet as nimble and graceful as a pianist's, unrolled the fabric. He grew lovingly impatient with my efforts to help but he had to put up with me for once again this was a task for at least two tall people. As we began to stretch the material out I saw that it was loosely woven but strong like nylon cord in automobile tires. It felt as indestructible as a child-proof bottle of aspirin, but it was as porous as a kitchen sieve.

"John, this will never work," I said. "Look, the sun will go right through it."

"Maybe. Maybe not."

We got it hung from the trellis he had installed the day before. Gently he let it fall over the window and hang there in the hot stillness of the summer morning. He secured the bottom with a lath and a couple of small nails.

"Come on inside," he ordered, as he nimbly scooted down the ladder, mostly frontward.

We went in. The room was shaded but not darkened. Mitchell snapped off the lamp we had focussed on the card game. Conclusively.

"Look!" exclaimed Elizabeth. "You can see through it!"

Sure enough. This white fabric turned away the sun but it was so openly woven that from inside the house you could clearly see the oleander bushes and the cherry tree in the backyard. But even more distinct was the faraway lofty summit of Mt. St. Helena.

"Thank you, John," Elizabeth said, looking up at the tall man, modestly pleased with himself. "Thanks especially for the mountain. I had really dreaded this summer."

So the "Master Suite" with the queen-size bed and the cluttered desk and the row of memory-laden artifacts on the window sill was made comfortable for the worst of the summer months. I often had to sneak in and turn on the air conditioner long before Elizabeth felt it was necessary. But if I did, with John Mitchell's miracle fabric and the Pacific Gas and Electric feeding the air conditioner, the room we both loved was made hospitable even for this long hot season of Elizabeth's endurance.

One morning, soon after the white fabric was in place, I was astounded to find the air conditioner on soon after breakfast, long before I would have turned on the switch. I started to comment on this unusual occurrence, but thought better of it. Elizabeth would be sure it was an instance of indirect communication, an unhealthy family communication style. We both grew up in households skilled at it. She would be sure I was tactfully suggesting that she was using too much electricity. But it was odd that she would turn the air conditioner on so very early in the day. My anxiety was eased later that day and quite forgotten when Elizabeth expressed enthusiasm for our weekly shopping event planned for the following day.

CHAPTER 22

Aaron and Hur Held Up His Hands So They Were Steady Until Sunset

It was another hot summer day. The venerable blue pick-up truck, with the air conditioner going full blast, made its way up the valley to the Sonoma County dump like a homing pigeon. Six years had passed since a similar trip with Mother's big sofa. The two dogs who had accompanied us on that earlier trip, the descendents by adoption of the dogs we brought from Georgia and Connecticut, had both died. The last of the two to die was Sheba, a large black standard poodle whom Elizabeth rescued from a divorcing couple. Sheba took ill suddenly one Sunday afternoon. Her personal veterinarian, generous Max Powers, practiced miles away. He kindly agreed to see her if we could bring her to his establishment on Broadway in downtown Oakland. We were greatly relieved and glad to make the trip if Max could help Sheba.

When we arrived, the first thing he wanted was a urine sample. It was remarkable that the traffic did not come to a total standstill as we followed Sheba around, our eyes focussed unblinkingly on every sniff, and my posture poised in an anticipatory stoop, as she sought an appropriate place to oblige the vet . . . and us. The problem Sheba faced was nothing compared to mine. Elizabeth, more an expert in such matters than I, was full of advice as to how this should be done, but the doing was up to me as it took a degree of flexibility and agility which Elizabeth no longer possessed.

The problem was to slip up quietly behind Sheba with a small carton in your hand without alarming her and shutting off the flow. This would be hard enough to do even if you were not convulsed with laughter and self-conciously aware of a growing gallery of spectators.

Although we actually succeeded in getting the specimen, Sheba was beyond even the skilled help of Max Powers. When she died we reluctantly sought no replacement for we didn't want to send Abby, the indoor cat, into shock. We also had two good outdoor cats, Ivan and Beatrice, excellent gopher hunters, and we didn't want to discourage them. When we discovered that Ivan needed a hysterectomy, we tried to change her name. But she resisted. So she remained Ivan.

She was allowed in the house only to come into our dressing room, which has an outside door, when we were preparing for bed. Ivan would lope into the room and go straight to Elizabeth where she would knead and suck at Elizabeth's thick cotton bathrobe. It was a nightly ritual as Elizabeth talked with her and stroked her luxuriant black coat. Elizabeth felt Ivan had been separated from her mother too early in life. After a few minutes, Ivan was content to leave and bounded away happily when she was dismissed. Abby kept her distance during this one time of day when Ivan was granted house privileges.

Now we were heading once more to the Sonoma County dump. As the dogs had not been replaced and the cats resisted travel, there were neither dogs or cats with us in the truck. Our new friend, the green oxygen tank, secured with the middle seat belt, stood up between us in the generous cab. We had a small load for the dump and then were going on to Healdsburg to do our Fourth of July shopping.

Of all the problems we faced in the role reversal foisted on us by Elizabeth's illness, few compared with the stress produced by turning the regular household shopping over to me. I hated to shop. We made out the shopping list together and I knew what I was to get, but I hated the actual act of shopping. Therefore, my goal was to get it over with as quickly as possible. So I would rush through the aisles, grab the first item which seemed reasonably near what we wanted, regardless of cost or qualifications, and hurry home. One day at a "control burn" session Elizabeth confessed how aggravated and sometimes angry she was whenever I came home from shopping.

"You never read the labels. You bring home trout on which the date has expired. You bring home grapefruit canned in sugar instead of natural juice. You never look at the specials. You spend twice as much money as you need to." She was really upset. It caught me by surprise. I had no idea. She was always so reluctant to criticize my domestic skills that words of grievance ordinarily stuck in her throat. But these complaints poured out. Had it not been for the "control burn" hour, I suspect she would have suffered in silence and never said a word, building up for a wide-ranging blaze. But now, she more than spoke. To my utter dismay, I saw actual tears in her eyes when she looked down at the rumpled grocery list I had brought back to her. With painful bemusement she whispered, "I never realized how much I really enjoyed the grocery shopping."

So we went to work on that problem. Healdsburg, slightly larger and slightly farther from us than Calistoga, had an enormous and beautiful new Safeway store. Although we always tried to patronize Calistoga merchants, one day when I was in that new Safeway I realized that the aisles were wide enough to accommodate a wheelchair without blocking traffic. If I could get Elizabeth to agree to use the wheelchair we had borrowed from the church for emergencies, I could push her around in it and she could do the shopping. Much to my amazement, she agreed at once to this proposal. But after a few tries, I realized that something was wrong. She didn't seem to enjoy it much, and I was short-tempered as the pusher.

So once again, we discussed the tension fairly objectively and dispassionately in a "control burn" session. We discovered that we had conflicting goals. It reminded me of faculty quarrels which sometimes go on for years until the factions face up to the fact that they really have different goals so how can they agree on curriculum or admissions or much of anything!

So it was with us. I wanted to get the shopping done as quickly as possible. Elizabeth wanted to do the shopping as thoroughly as possible. They were mutually exclusive goals. I did not understand the importance of reading the fine print on the labels or comparing prices or looking for generic products. She did not understand that I hadn't planned on spending the whole afternoon in Healdsburg! Once she had agreed to the wheelchair, we assumed we were cooperating in a common task. But that cooperation was shattered by conflicting methodology. Mine was speed at all costs. Hers was thoroughness to protect quality and save costs. Once we got that straightened out and I slowed down the speed of the wheelchair and entered into the spirit of her style of shopping, and got my mind and schedule set for a leisurely time, the wheelchair shopping became a harmonious, delightful and productive event.

It sounds like such a trivial thing, but it was something we could do together, it kept Elizabeth involved where she was the expert, and it provided many of the warmest moments we had in those years. She appeared to lose her reluctance to be seen in a wheelchair and we moved up and down aisles, laughing and arguing and visiting with passers-by who might easily guess that we were having a good time. The "control burn" had transformed dreaded shopping into a mirthful happening.

So now we were on the way to the dump and afterwards to do the grocery shopping. What a beautiful prospect, even without the dogs! However, this excursion had a cloud hanging over it. We were getting ready for our traditional Fourth of July celebration. But this year it would be dreadfully different.

Years before I had been invited to Perth, Western Australia, as a consultant. Elizabeth accompanied me and we had a cordial time with new Australian friends. At the same time, a couple from the Berkeley church, important members of the "little family of the heart" for scores of people, Margie and Barrett Coates, were in Brisbane to visit their daughter and her husband. So it came about that we arranged to meet in Adelaide and travelled to the Outback, Ayers Rock, Sydney, New Zealand and Fiji together. Such joint travelling is a good way to break or make friendships. We were lucky. Each of us discovered he or she could tolerate each other's warts. Every summer after that trip we celebrated the Fourth together. We made a delightful ritual of attending the old-fashioned, small town, Fourth of July parade in Calistoga with whatever family or other friends we could corral or just the four of us.

Elizabeth had not gone to the parade since the arrival of the green oxygen tank. Then last year Barrett arrived with the borrowed wheelchair in the back of his station wagon. He announced he was going to take Elizabeth to the parade. In his charming, free-wheeling, gentle but determined way, he did just that. There was a special camaraderie between Barrett and Elizabeth. His feet hurt, too. He had stepped on a land mine at Omaha Beach and spent months in army hospitals getting his feet to function again. He was often in great discomfort, especially when he was tired, but never said a word. He was too busy earning a living as an actuary and discovering and sharing an incredible joy in just being alive as he made old player pianos work again, restored fine furniture, gently prodded a tremendously extended family up every steep trail in the Sierra, and made excellent wine in his cellar from grapes which scores of friends stomped out in his backyard.

Barrett was very persuasive. Elizabeth was very vulnerable. The vibrations between them suggested unspoken understanding and mutual respect. So when time came to go to the parade, Elizabeth was ready. She wore a very large hat. Barrett wore a T-shirt bearing some friendly message. We parked the car as near the parade route as we could and Barrett unloaded the wheelchair. He would not let me assist in any way. This was his project. As Margie and I watched in delighted amazement, the two of them went sailing down the sidewalk and claimed our usual spot alongside a Mexican restaurant to participate in the parade, not simply watch it. No one just "watches" the Calistoga Fourth of July parade!

It began, as it has for decades, with local dignitaries periously poised high above the back seats of polished convertibles followed by splendid horses, bridled with silver on leather. Next in the noisy line came ancient fire wagons and then Brownies and Girl Scouts on flatbed trucks cooling themselves in a plastic pool. The parade stretched on with a wonderfully long line of model A Fords and ancient Packards and pre-adolescent twirling girls and bewildered children and Shriners and water squirting volunteer firemen and other cultural delights beyond recent imagination.

It was a wonderful parade that year, it was a wonderful Fourth. Barrett made it so for Elizabeth and for all of us. Barrett and Margie left a few days later for ten days hiking in the high Sierra. And there in the beautiful mountains he loved, death came to Barrett, suddenly, as he prepared in the bright early morning sun for another day of living which he enjoyed and made so bright and beautiful for others.

During the year which had passed since the previous July with the delightful Fourth and the shattering death, Margie had been a most welcomed and especially helpful guest in our home. Elizabeth and she grew very close during those months. Barrett's death opened up conversation which Elizabeth had seldom encouraged. She was reaching out with her loving and intuitive gifts to ease some of Margie's grief. She talked with her of her first husband's drowning and the difficulty she had in accepting his death especially in the absence of a recovered body. She told Margie of her present concerns for me and explained that she worried about dying not in fear of death but out of reluctance to leave me and the children. So the year had been a time of shared concern between the two women and the effort to be helpful to one another. Margie spent many nights at our house. She was generous in making it easier for me to be away for more than a few hours. If her grief found some outlet and healing in being needed, then there was a practical service even in Elizabeth's weakening condition.

We were scarcely home from the Healdsburg shopping trip when Margie arrived for this more sober celebration of the Fourth. Still she came, as she had for many years, loaded down with far more than her share of provisions. She never brought ordinary stuff. The food was usually something different, imaginative, delicious—except when she was trying to honor some diet one of us was almost always trying to follow. She was very close to a lot of young people and among the treasures she brought there was always some banner to fly or youthful fad to enjoy. The holiday passed with some pleasure and satisfaction as we talked freely about last year and Elizabeth's debut in the wheelchair which subsequently had proven so helpful in solving the shopping problem. The most poignant moment came when we hung a boldly colored wind sock on a post near the small rose garden and dedicated it to Barrett. We allowed ourselves to remember how we had joked that if all four of us were to be buried in that small rose garden we would have to be laid to rest spoon fashion.

So the holiday came and went but the summer felt endless with its heat. We enjoyed the shaded window in the bedroom and Elizabeth consumed enough ice to support a family of penguins. One day I came home to find her visiting with a young woman from Berkeley whose father was running a nearby errand. After she left, Elizabeth said to me very quietly as I got up to go to the kitchen, "I'm half blind. I can't see out of my left eye."

"What?" I said, turning abruptly from my errand. "You can't see?"

"Nothing with that eye."

"What happened?" I asked.

"I don't know. While Mary Jane was visiting with me, I realized something was wrong."

"What did you do?"

"I didn't do anything. I waited for you to come home mostly."

We called Frank immediately. He seemed to sense right away what the problem might be. After about 45 minutes, Elizabeth's vision returned but it faded again once or twice in the following days before we finished the rounds, seeing the ophthalmologist, the radiologist and the surgeon. Frank's diagnosis was correct: amaurosis fugax. Elizabeth declined the remedy of surgery which had mixed endorsers. And the problem returned only once again. It was such uncertainties which made it difficult for me to be away.

CHAPTER 23

But on the Seventh Day You Shall Rest

For many months I had planned to go to New York City for a few days early in August. A two day meeting had been scheduled for a committee of the national church. In order to take advantage of the lowest air fare, I had arranged "to stay over Saturday night." There were many good reasons to go. It was a small committee and the date had been settled for many months. The business to be done was important. And I had looked forward to the extra day in New York to visit our daughter who had recently moved into the city from Long Island. I also felt I needed a change of scenery. I would be gone from Wednesday morning to Sunday evening.

Alas, there were also many reasons not to go. Elizabeth had had a persistent infection on her ankle bone. The infection cleared after many weeks but the wound did not heal. Frank began treating the wound with something used for burns, healing from the inside out. The wound had to be tended every day and he helped us set up a little routine to take care of it.

Every night before we went to bed we had this intimate little medical ritual in our dressing room. Elizabeth sat in the chair and I sat cross-legged on the carpet before her. Ivan, the outdoor cat, who was allowed into our dressing room each evening just for the time we spent getting ready for bed, was there. Just the three of us. Ivan would climb around the closets happily but usually soon gravitated to Elizabeth to receive her evening mothering.

I put all the equipment we needed, gauze, adhesive tape, little cotton balls on sticks to probe the "hole" we were trying to fill with new flesh, hydrogen peroxide, sterile pads, everything—I put it all in a box and stored it under the bathroom sink. I would settle myself down on the carpet, pull out the little box from under the sink behind me, spread the equipment out, lift Elizabeth's foot gently into my lap and go to work.

"Remember the foot-washing service?" Elizabeth asked one night as we began this evening task.

"How could I forget it."

One summer we had worked with a refresher course for ministers and their husbands and wives (I think then there was only one acknowledged minister's husband!) at our church. Lay people were involved—as teachers and guinea pigs! The course of study for the week was designed to close with a worship service. One of the ministers, skilled in liturgical matters, volunteered to take charge. He arranged a foot-washing ceremony in accordance with New Testament tradition. Tradition or not, it was new to almost everyone there. We approached it with a good deal of curiosity and anxiety. It proved to be a very effective and moving event.

"Do you remember what we learned?" Elizabeth asked.

At once I knew what she was thinking about for it had impressed us both deeply . . . rebuked us. We had acknowledged to each other that we found it far easier to get down on our knees and wash our neighbor's feet, as the Service required, than to sit quietly and allow our neighbor to get down before us and wash our feet, as the Service also required.

"Yes. O yes, I do. I remember well," I said.

"Well?" she said with a rising inflection which suggested that any numbskull would understand what she was thinking.

"'Well what?" I said with vague annoyance.

"Did it ever occur to you," Elizabeth replied, "that I'm the one getting her feet washed now?"

I sat there silently for a moment, looking up at her, already feeling like an insensitive clod.

"Is it really that hard for you?" I finally asked her.

"I don't have much choice, do I?"

"But can you believe it that I enjoy these few minutes every night about as much as any part of the day."

"Well, it *is* intimate," she replied, "if you go for one-way intimacy."

"You have never let me help you with your feet before. In all these years that you have had to nurse them along day by day you've never let me help."

"I would never have let you even see them if I could have helped it."

"You don't seem to try to hide your hands."

"What's the use. I long ago gave up on hiding them. But my feet! They are repulsive. Even to me."

I lifted her foot up a few inches out of my lap with the heel resting in the palm of my hand. I looked at it closely. Scars from some unremarkable surgery twenty years ago crisscrossed it. One toe was bent under and quite hidden between two others. The nails, thick and cracked.

Elizabeth tried to free her foot from my grasp. It was as though my steady looking at it had begun to burn it like a heat lamp left on too long. But I held on firmly and she gave up her resistance.

I thought of the $280 pair of shoes a miracle shoemaker, a recent immigrant, we guessed, from Brazil had made for her. We had found him in a crowded family-wearied store-front shop on a side street in Vallejo. We had been led to him by a series of "coincidences." His waiting room was an old sofa with broken springs shoved up against the unwashed plate glass store window. On our first exploratory visit there was a husky young man also waiting. He told us he was a highway patrol officer. He had been terribly smashed three years earlier while making an arrest on Interstate 80. "I was in a wheelchair until last May . . . wouldn't be walking at all today if it weren't for this cobbler," he explained. "The old 'Portugee' has got it in his fingers. He could fit you blind."

'The old Portugee' did the same for Elizabeth. The day she put on that pair of shoes was Liberation Day in our household. Those blessed shoes, resoled a hundred times, enabled her to get around for years. She even kept them beside her bed at night to help her if she got up. It had been a long time since she could walk barefooted. That pair of shoes was still in daily use. How scruffy they had come to look and how hard I tried to clean them up for her. We finally got a second pair which she seldom wore. They were made of deep mahogany cordovan. I found a small dressy purse to match. But purse and shoes alike languished in her closet. She said she was saving them for something special. I suspect the second pair which was more costly than the first were not as comfortable and she didn't want me to be disappointed.

I still held her foot. She looked resigned to whatever I planned to do with it. Finally, I spoke. "Look, Elizabeth, look at that foot. Think what it has done. If it looks a little tired, it has earned it. It has chased dogs down Broadway in Oakland and kids over the rocks at Pemaquid. It's pushed the brake on the car hundreds of times just in the Safeway parking lot without ever letting you have an accident except, of course, for the time you rear-ended that Jaguar on Marin Avenue." The family never let her forget her only accident in years of driving. She smiled—just a little—but I was not through.

I touched her foot gently and went on. "It's carted you around the house feeding and caring for your folks. How many trays did you carry for your Dad . . . and your Mother, too, up and down that treacherous staircase in the Ashby Avenue house. Never once did that foot give out and let you fall. How many students and faculty and committees, the appreciative ones and the ingrates alike, have you fed. Think of the discouraged clergy types who have received more than gourmet beans at your table . . . and all those vagrants our kids brought home, lovers and loners! Give your foot a break. Both of them! They've done you well . . . and me, too."

Ivan, the cat, had now made it to Elizabeth's lap. Elizabeth was stroking her silky black fur softly with her twisted hand.

"But still . . . still it is *you*," she said with a quiet intense voice, imploring my understanding. "It is always you, you . . . on your knees . . . never me. That's the hardest thing of all."

I was uneasy with the urgency in her feeling. I was trying to persuade her . . . argue with her, for her . . . and all she wanted was for me to listen, listen, listen . . . and not always have a solution. What solution was there anyway? If there was one it was not in my wisdom . . . nor in Job's.

"Hell," I said with a half-way smile, "I'm not on my knees. I'm on my butt!"

I thought this conversation was over. I hoped so. I had struck out again. But Elizabeth was not through. I could tell she was still troubled.

"But if you go to New York next week . . . "

"Yes?"

"Who will you ask to stay with me? I wish you would let me stay alone. But I know you won't. Do you think Margie would come again? We've leaned on her so much."

"Would you let her help with your ankle?"

"I hate to ask anyone. But Margie is no stranger to foot problems. I think Barrett suffered more with his feet than he ever let on. At least, I never stepped on a land mine."

The cat hopped down and then came back and started kneading at Elizabeth's bathrobe and nursing at it. Elizabeth remarked again that she thought we had taken Ivan away from her mother too early.

After a while I said, "Time to go to bed, Ivan." I opened the sliding screen out to our little private deck and Ivan ran out as pleased to go as she had been to come in. Could it only be so for us.

* * * * * * * *

I went to New York.

Margie came—spontaneous, package-ladened Margie—still bruised by her own grief. She knew what a private person Elizabeth was. They had been friends for years but not once had Elizabeth ever talked to her about her arthritis or now her lung disease until she was moved to do so in helping Margie with her own grief. Margie dressed the wound in Elizabeth's ankle, so Elizabeth told me later, as though she had been caring for broken feet for years, casually, carefully. "No big thing."

When I was free on Saturday I took a Fifth Avenue bus from the uptown hotel where I was staying. It was a bright warm summer day like many I had thoroughly enjoyed when attending summer school there exactly forty years earlier. I thought I would ride the bus to Washington Square and walk around the Village before making my way at noon to my daughter's apartment in what is euphemistically called the East Village instead of the Lower East Side.

But before I got to Washington Square I saw the array of Fifth Avenue stores and remembered my first Christmas in New York and how proud I had been to buy gifts there for my "rustic" relatives like Aunt Jenny or my parents in Colorado. Now I wanted to get a "thank you" gift for Margie and something special for Elizabeth. With a Fifth Avenue label!

I got off the bus and walked into B. Altman's. I couldn't believe my eyes. It hadn't changed a bit. It smelled the same way, wax and perfumery. And those beautiful floors, highly polished hardwood. Imagine the upkeep. The glass display cases framed with red mahogany and filled with jewelry or cosmetics or leather goods all shone like the passenger compartment of a classic Rolls Royce. I quickly found the gift Elizabeth and I had talked about for Margie. It was a leather money belt for her to use on a trip she was planning for the fall to Egypt with caring friends who had invited her to join them.

For Elizabeth I wanted to get a house coat or dress. Something she could wear comfortably in the house, loose and open, yet with long sleeves and plenty full to accommodate the oxygen tube. An old-fashioned "floor walker" sent me to an upper floor where I found an immense department full of such dresses.

The store had just opened for the day and there were not many customers around early on a summer Saturday morning. Not many clerks either. I found something displayed on a model that I rather liked. There was a well-dressed woman fingering similar garments nearby.

"Would one wear a dress like this outside your own home?" I asked her after catching her eye.

"Well," she said, over the rims of her casually placed glasses, looking down at the garment I held toward her tentatively, "one might wear it in one's garden." She even corrected my grammar.

I made no further inquiry of that New York matron.

I decided against that particular dress but found another one, hanging in a rack, which I liked. There was only one clerk visible to me. She was a small older woman, lively and nimble. She seemed omnipresent, darting everywhere through those many racks of informal clothes. I took it to the desk around which she was at the moment hovering. As she moved toward me I fancied that it was the actress who plays Sophia, the blunt "little old lady," in "The Golden Girls." She wasn't, of course, but the more I dealt with her the more I thought she could be!

She was wearing soft soled flat shoes. I wondered that such a fashionable store would allow such informality. I imagined that her feet hurt and she could hardly wait to retire.

"You must get weary before the day is over with all that running around," I said to her solicitously.

"Not really," she said. "I'm not as old as I look. I try to look old. The customers are more patient. I'm nowhere near eligible for Social Security. What can I do for you?"

"I'm thinking about this dress or housecoat or whatever you call it for my wife."

"Is she as small as I am?"

"Or smaller."

"Well, take a look," she replied. With one big sweep she threw the dress over her head and pulled it down over her clothes. "I wonder if you like the neck."

The neck was awful. It was very wide and hung down her shoulders halfway to her elbows.

"Oh that will never do," I said. "I'm sorry to have troubled you. But thanks. It would look like . . . well, she never could have worn it but she wouldn't have wanted to say so. I'm from California and I don't want to have to return what I buy if I can avoid it. I hate all the wrapping and mailing and negotiating."

"I know what you mean. That one would not have done, I'm sure. Go find something else," she said. "Try that rack by the window. And watch the neckline. Little women can't afford too much opening or a lot of broad heavy lines at the neck."

With that she pulled the rejected dress up over her head and off. Then she hustled off to return it to its place. And I went over to the rack by the window. At once I saw just the right thing. It had a subdued over all pattern in summer colors, but what sold me was a sassy ten inch gathered flounce around the bottom. The only formal dress Elizabeth ever bought after we were married had such a feature. She only wore it once. To a fancy University affair at the Palace Hotel in San Francisco. I loved the way it swirled when she walked . . . in heels . . . a long long time ago.

I took the dress with the flounce back to the friendly clerk. "Here. What do you think of this?" I asked.

"Do you want me to model it for you?" "Sophia" responded with a naughty smile.

"Thanks. I'd love that, but I really think it is just right."

"I know it would fit me," she said, "and look good, too. The neck is just right."

"I like the ruffle or whatever on the skirt."

"Oh, yes," she said, pulling the skirt out to its fullness. "I can see your little lady twirling over the floor and out into your arms on your California patio."

She caught me unprepared. It was like a surprise blow to the solar plexus. This little lady looked up at my silence, anticipating a rejoiner. "Oh, yes, so can I," I said at last. And I turned from her as she wrote up the ticket and put a little bow on the box.

Despite the brief reunion with my daughter and her family, the rest of that long long Saturday so far from our valley dragged on and on. The night was worse. The next morning I was ready to leave the hotel long before it was necessary, but I felt somehow if I kept on moving, I would get home sooner. I took a taxi to the West Side terminal. It sailed so fast down the empty avenue washed by the early Sunday sun that I decided I would splurge.

"Go ahead," I said to the driver. "Take me all the way to the Newark airport."

It was a quiet morning and he was glad to oblige. The gods are with me, I thought, for I arrived so early at the airport that when I checked in the clerk invited me to consider an earlier flight. I got a window seat with no one else beside me. The day was purely clear, cleansed perhaps by the same wind which we were told would push us to an early arrival in the Bay Area. But I could not relax or sleep and I began to greet each acceleration in my homeward journey with increased concern. What Providence is speeding me home?

I did not call home when I arrived on the ground in San Francisco. I seldom did if I were early because Elizabeth knew how long it took me to drive home. Then if I were delayed she would worry. Now my good fortune continued. The parking lot shuttle bus was just pulling around the terminal drive as I came out into the California noontime sun. I jumped aboard. I got my car without any hindrance except the pleasant surprise of having the parking lot fee-taker ask for my ID when I claimed the Senior discount!

The stoplights on 19th Avenue through San Francisco seem synchronized to favor me and even the Sunday traffic in Golden Gate Park was very obliging. I sped over the Golden Gate bridge with a nostalic nod in the direction of the East Bay. I caught a glance of the Campanile. Between it and me was the Bay itself playing host to hundreds of Sunday sailors and their sails all also bending before the push of a beneficent wind.

The traffic did not slow even on the Waldo grade, and the tunnel's rainbow arches seemed to broaden to let me pass, on up Highway 101 past all the familiar exits to San Rafael and Novato and Petaluma and Rohnert Park, right on through Santa Rosa to the Mark West Springs exit. On to the Franz Valley Road cut off and up that winding narrow grade until just over the top of the first long hill Mt. St. Helena came into view. All down hill now, down past the Kettlewells and the fancy cow barn made into a contemporary house when cattle gave way to grapes, down through the tunnel of trees and out into Knights' Valley and Spencer Lane and out across the highway and the sharp turn to our driveway marked by the mailbox. Across the bridge. I pulled into the yard with the gravel pinging. I thought surely they would hear me and Margie would come to the door, but there was no sign of anyone.

I was eager to give my gifts. I was also eager to receive the gift Elizabeth always had ready for me, indisputable evidence in her face and in her voice that life could begin again for her now that I was home. Was it for these gifts that I had hurried as though they were so fragile they would not keep one extra hour? Or . . . I walked into the house and called. I heard no one. As I moved down the corridor toward our bedroom, I passed the oxygen machine. The tubing lead me into the bedroom and on through to the dressing room.

"Oh, look who's here!" It was Elizabeth.

"Surprise?" said Margie. "We weren't expecting you for hours."

"We got caught, Margie," said Elizabeth.

"We sure did," explained Margie. "We were lazy last night and decided to wait until this morning to dress Elizabeth's ankle."

"Give me a kiss," said Elizabeth. "And then we will finish up. Margie is wonderful with the feet."

I kissed Elizabeth gently, briefly, and gave Margie a hug.

As they turned back to the ankle, I went out to the car to get my gear and the gifts.

Margie was extravagant in appreciation for the money belt. I felt we really had made a good selection. Elizabeth didn't say much about the dress. But after Margie left she surprised me by asking me to help her try it on. It really did fit and she looked lovely in it. I think she felt so.

"Now I have something to wear for our dinner party," she said at last. "I'm really glad that you invited them now that I have something pretty to wear." That was high praise from Elizabeth and I was well rewarded. I was especially pleased that she sounded enthusiastic about our bold plans to entertain.

CHAPTER 24

Is Not the Body More than the Clothing?

lizabeth sympathetically suggested that I was wasting time and energy even to think about making a pie crust. "Get a frozen one," she said. "They have good ones at Cal Mart. Just be sure it says on the label 'all butter'."

We were in the midst of harmonious collaboration on a very special dinner party. We had invited old friends, Dick and Mary Hafner, who were now neighbors in Alexander Valley, to meet Angie and Frank Mueller. It was a bold undertaking. Mary Hafner once taught French cooking and the Muellers don't even buy bread at the grocery store!

The week before, I had sent Frank word that I sensed Elizabeth would welcome an opportunity to talk with him alone. So when I went with her for her next appointment, I made an excuse to absent myself. On the way home she said with a bit of gaiety in her voice, "Well now, I've talked with my psychiatrist and I feel fine."

"Good," I said.

"Good, indeed," she replied. "He really knows how to listen. Also he gave me another pill to take."

When the evening of the dinner party rolled around, our life felt put together in good fashion, better than in months. The new dress was very becoming and Elizabeth seemed to me to swirl around in it like a young woman newly in love. At the dinner party Frank sat on her right and Dick on her left; she was

166

burnished and beaming as hostess and wife. And the pie! It was a wonder. Into the "all butter" crust I pushed softened vanilla ice cream into which I had dumped fragments of lemon peel. Then froze it hard again. I had the plates ice cold and placed the pieces of pie on them into little puddles of raspberry puree with fresh raspberries on top. The chef was much pleased by the guests' response! As a dinner party, this event was somewhat different from the catered surprise party years earlier.

"Look at Elizabeth tonight," I whispered to Frank. "You must be a very good psychiatrist."

He nodded agreement that she was in excellent form but then added, "I suspect it is the new medicine."

Alas! Within a week or two the shine was gone. The edema which Frank and Elizabeth had fought for years as a mortal enemy was gaining the upper hand. Lasix, Zaroxolyn and Maxide had become household words for us, but they were demanding larger and larger doses to justify their place in the resisting army.

For many weeks Elizabeth had had a regular Tuesday appointment at Frank's office. On one September Tuesday he said to her, "Could you do me a favor?"

"Of course," she replied, "if I possibly can."

"I know it will take a lot out of you. But could you possibly go back to Santa Rosa and see the cardiologist again?" He looked at her with clear eyes, their very cleanness somehow seeming to hide the feeling he dared not express. "I know it is a lot to ask, but I've grown so fond of you . . . I fear I've lost my objectivity. I need to have you see Dr. Price for my sake."

"I have been back several times," Elizabeth said.

"Yes, I know," Frank replied.

There was a deep silence in that small examining room, an age of silence which felt as though it covered all the days and weeks and years of visits there with that young physician. At last Elizabeth simply said: "Will you make the appointment or shall I?"

Two days later, Thursday, I wheeled Elizabeth into the waiting room of James Price, M.D., in Santa Rosa. It was there, more than five years earlier, that I felt I had deposited all reasonable hope when I settled with the office bookkeeper and no return appointment was suggested. We had left that day counting on two more years of life for Elizabeth and hoping for three. It had already been more than five. This day they were waiting for us and were obviously prepared to avoid unnecessary delay. Dr. Price saw Elizabeth at once and after a time invited me to join them.

He appeared older to me than I had remembered. He was older. I wondered what had happened to him in five years. Did he look older because we needed him to be older? I think not. We had learned differently about doctors and age in the six years with Frank Mueller.

"There are some invasive measures we could take, Mrs. Barr," he began, "which might prolong your life. Of course you would have to go to the hospital."

"No," Elizabeth said clearly. "I do not want that."

Dr. Price seemed to relax. "I am glad to hear you say that," he said. "Sometimes people feel 'specialists' are magicians and they come here with expectations we can't meet."

"I am here," Elizabeth said, "only because Dr. Mueller wanted me to come. We are not here going over his head."

"I understand," Dr. Price continued ambiguously, "and I hope you will not misunderstand me, but I could only wish that we could provide as well for other patients. I feel you are ideally situated for your condition. Better than any hospital can offer, I suspect."

"What do you mean?" I asked, trusting my voice at last.

He did not seem to hear me. He continued speaking to Elizabeth as though I were not there, as though it was her decision, her life. "You have one of the finest primary physicians in the area, one who is willing to make calls at your home. He tells me you have a beautiful spot in the country which you love and a husband who cares. Go home . . . go home and enjoy it all."

Elizabeth and I looked at each other. I stirred as though to get up.

"Go home and come back and surprise us again," the doctor continued. "You have surprised us already you know."

So once more we left the cardiologists' office. Once more I left hope, a much smaller package of hope, at their bookkeeper's window. Elizabeth asked me to stop when we reached the outside corridor which was a third story balcony around the atrium of this modern professionals' building. I thought she only wanted to rest a moment. Perhaps she did. But she motioned me to push the wheelchair nearer the edge of the balcony. Once more she admired the immense plant growing there in the atrium. She admired it closely and silently. Then she told me its Latin name and expressed surprise that it was doing so well in that environment. It somehow felt like a re-run.

We took the elevator downstairs and moved slowly out into the intense heat of the September afternoon. As Elizabeth was moving from the chair into the car she stopped. "Look," she said, "there's a twenty dollar bill."

I picked it up. "There's no way to find its owner," I said.

"Not unless someone comes along and claims it right away," Elizabeth answered. "Save it for the 'Bread for the World' offering. The first Sunday of October . . . Put it in for me." So I folded it into the back of my billfold.

I wondered if this were an opening. Did she want to talk? Was she thinking that her death was imminent? I had thought so earlier but I did not think so now. I thought Dr. Price was saying, "We are having a beautiful Fall, enjoy it. Enjoy it at home even if it takes a few days or weeks from your life." I did not need to wonder much longer what Elizabeth was thinking for she turned and looked at me and asked me in very straightforward fashion, "Did you notice how he asked me the question about the invasive measures, about extending my life?"

"How do you mean?" I asked as we pulled out into the traffic of Sonoma Avenue and started home.

"I mean he didn't ask *us*. He didn't ask you," she responded as though she regarded that as a great curiosity.

"I suppose he felt it wasn't finally anyone else's business. You know we come into this world alone and we leave it alone," I said.

"I've heard you say that before," Elizabeth responded.

"I am sure you have," I answered soberly. "You have probably heard me call it 'existential terror.' That's what it is to me."

"I don't know what that means," she said. "I do remember that you called birth and death moments of 'ultimate loneliness.' I understand that and I couldn't disagree with you more!"

"I'm glad of that," I said.

"I just don't agree," she said in a quiet, determined, non-argumentative tone of voice. "I just don't feel that way. 'Jesus, Lover of my Soul,'" she quoted the familiar hymn. "How can we ever be truly alone in the whole universe? I guess there is too much Southern Baptist in me still."

"That's what you said once when you explained to me how much keeping a promise meant to you."

"Did I really?" she asked.

"Indeed you did. How could I forget. It changed lots for me. It kept us together."

"That's nice to hear," she said almost to herself alone. "Without promises who could face the future. That's what we build on. Marriages or . . . ." She stopped. It was clear she was through despite the rising inflection in her voice.

"Maybe you can rescue me from my existential terror," I said with a smile.

"Ultimate aloneness . . . or loneliness?" she asked reflectively. "That's what you said. I just don't feel that way."

"How do you feel?"

"Ultimate intimacy I guess. If you want big words," she replied. "But it's very simple. Don't laugh at me."

"You know I won't. I need to hear," I said.

"About being alone when you die?" she asked.

"Yes," I replied.

She did not reply at once. I knew she would in time. We were both looking straight ahead. Right down Franz Valley Road. And not really seeing it at all.

Finally Elizabeth spoke to me . . . to us, "I just feel that as long as I am alive you will hold my hand on this side. And when I am dead, Jesus will hold my hand on the other side. He promised that. I really believe it. I'll never be lonely. Just please don't let go on this side . . . too soon."

The tears popped out of my eyes as though her words had spontaneously punctured little balloons full of water which fell down my face until I tasted the salt and had to stop the car to dry them and to touch her and look at her and see the road ahead again.

"I promise," I said after a very long silence, a silence so full I could not invade it with words for fear everything beautiful in our life together might spill out and be gone forever. "I'll hang on tight."

She looked up at me appreciatively, but was very matter-of-fact about it all. "You know," she went on, "I'm glad I've come to love 'Jesu, Joy of Man's Desiring' for I haven't dared sing some of the hymns I grew up with since you and your friends made fun of them in New Haven. Not aloud, anyway. But, I've kept on humming them to myself just the same. I discovered the other day that I remember almost all the words to 'What a Friend We have in Jesus.' She hummed a line or two with a few words breaking out, "Precious Savior, still our refuge, Take it to the Lord in prayer." I do pretty well with 'Jesus, Lover of my Soul,' too. 'Jesus, Lover of my soul, Let me to thy bosom fly.'"

She sounded relieved as though she had been wanting to tell me that for a long time. I started to reply, but she went right on. "You know," she said, "I've been talking to Jesus a lot lately. When I go out on that little deck off our dressing room, it isn't just to sneak a smoke." She smiled. "We visit there a lot, he and I."

I looked at her curiously but not critically.

"Don't look at me like that. You know that I know Jesus is not sitting on the deck there with me beside that pink petunia or even on a cloud somewhere over Mt. St. Helena. But it's easier if I think about him and see him, yes, and hear him, when I talk with God—and isn't he part of your Trinity?—that's lots better than trying to have a conversation with the wind in the trees. Or with the Creator. Or the Christ . . . Jesus, a person, has ears. And, you know, speaks English." She smiled but plunged right on as if there were no time to lose now that she had decided to tell me these secrets of her soul. "I will admit that sometimes his masculinity gets in the way. I need him sometimes to be a woman, a friend like Margie, but then I feel that's his problem."

"What do you talk with him about?" I asked.

"Mostly the children," she said. "I know they are all grown up, but there's not a day I don't wonder or worry about one of them. But its amazing. In a week it always seems to work out."

"Work out?" I asked.

"Yes," she said. "It works out that they all get equal time. Except they get cheated on the days I'm most worried about you or upset about some stupid thing the State Department is doing in South Africa. Jesus and I have lots to talk about."

"Do you ever talk with him about dying?"

She didn't answer at once. I began to hope she wouldn't. I felt I had intruded and wished I could call the question back.

"It's sort of strange," she said at last quietly, but her voice was not sombre, it was light and loving. "I really don't. Somehow whenever I even think about death or anything strange or new, he's just there. I feel him all around me. Don't be jealous, my love. But he's just there. The Everlasting Arms I guess. So close . . . . "
And her voice trailed off somewhere, somewhere beyond us.

We rode along in a comfortable silence. I thought about the big row we had had when we felt our relationship was falling apart in the early days of her illness. It was she who came up with the idea that we had been thinking too much, she said, about what was happening to her and not enough about what was happening to us. I guess she and Jesus had something going back then. And, maybe also, I mused, maybe way back when she resolved to keep the promise she had made on a summer afternoon in Maine: "in sickness and in health; until death we do part."

* * * * * * * *

Elizabeth was very weary when we arrived home. The edema had caused her legs to swell more than they ever had before. The trip had taken several hours on a hot day. It had been quite a while since she had had her feet up. But it was different. Ordinarily the swelling had not been painful, but now both her legs were giving her a lot of discomfort. She went to the shaded bedroom to rest but it was not long until she reappeared and joined me for a "Happy Hour" on the porch.

Margie was in and out that weekend, and Saturday night the persistently faithful friends who had helped Elizabeth feel comfortable about the oxygen tank in public joined us for supper which I suspect they provided although these days are blurred in my memory. We had other company, young colleagues from San Anselmo on Sunday. Also a troubled neighbor who just stopped by to visit with Elizabeth because she was feeling so low. The neighbor went home and wrote Elizabeth a note telling her how much the visit had meant to her. Gave her courage. It arrived in the mail the following Wednesday.

After they left, Elizabeth complained that her legs had become almost unbearably painful. I called Frank. His associate was "on call." She had treated Elizabeth for head wounds six months earlier when she had fallen backwards over Abby and the oxygen tube and hit a sharp corner of the stove. I had come home that night from a brief meeting to find Elizabeth cleaning up blood all over the kitchen floor. She did not think she needed a doctor. If she didn't, I did! When I got her to the doctor, it was this same young woman who patiently cut away the hair and skillfully put in a couple dozen stitches.

In this instance now of the painful legs, she suggested that we try some heat. Something went wrong although I felt we followed the instructions carefully. By Monday morning Elizabeth's legs were badly blistered. She would not let me call either of the doctors.

"Tomorrow is our regular appointment," she argued. "I don't want to pester them. You take special care of my ankle tonight so at least that part of me will be all clean and nice when we get there tomorrow."

So that night we had the ritual on the dressing room floor, everything from the peroxide to Ivan nursing on the skirts of Elizabeth's robe. The next afternoon when we got to Frank's parking lot, Elizabeth suggested she would have to use the wheelchair. That was a first. She had always walked in and out of that office. I knew her legs must be very painful, indeed.

Frank saw her in the little emergency room near the back entrance which we had to use because of the wheelchair. He invited his associate to join him. They looked at the blisters and the swelling of the tissue. They left the room, which was un-usual, and conferred briefly. Frank returned and gave Elizabeth some Lazix directly by injection, called the pharmacist for an ointment for her legs and suggested she take some codeine, which she had never needed before, when we got home.

We stopped by the pharmacy. The assistant pharmacist was practically in the parking lot with the prescription when we got there, suggesting to me that Frank had made another urgent call so we would not have to wait. The advantages of a small town! And of a physician who isn't afraid to enter into his patient's dis-tress. Then Elizabeth suggested that we drive home the long way.

"There is more color in the vineyards on that side of the valley," she said. "We are in no hurry."

"Fine with me," I said. "But actually I was wondering if we should call our guests not to come tonight." For many weeks, two couples who had been particularly supportive of Margie since Barrett's death, and who included her in their parties and trips, had arranged to bring her and a special dinner to share with us on this particular Tuesday night.

"No," Elizabeth said, much to my surprise, "I guess it is when you are hurting most you need people around who love you."

So we went the long way home. No hurry. We looked at the vines and applauded the packed full gondolas being rushed with their fragrant crops to the wineries. We commented on the fresh striping of the highway and talked about my scheduled trip for the next day, Wednesday, to Raphael House in San Francisco.

"I expect to have one of the best loads tomorrow I have ever had," I told her. "Frank Messmer and Helen Walka both called to ask what time I would be there so they could be sure I had some help loading their stuff. That sounds like they've got a lot. And that's only a beginning."

Finally we reached our driveway. The noisy gravel again welcomed us home. Elizabeth disconnected herself from the tank in the car and walked into the house, plugged into the other equipment and sat down at the table to rest. We were glad to be home. We decided Elizabeth would be more comfortable if she simply went to bed. That pleased Abby, the indoor cat, because it settled the question of where she would curl up for the evening. After they both were settled, I went out to the backyard with my pruning clippers and hunted for the finest red rose I could find. Our 'Futura' could not be beat this time of year. I chose a full but tight blossom and brought it in to Elizabeth.

"How beautiful," she said. She held it for a long time. I thought of her mother teaching me, unknowingly, how to look at a flower. Elizabeth had learned the same lesson. She held the rose gently by the stem between the thorns. She turned it slowly as though it were the whole universe in miniature, a gathered complex of love. "Please get that little crystal bud vase. I think it won't be too big. Then put it in the window. I can see it there. We can move it in the morning if it is too hot there."

Soon the folks arrived for dinner. I began wondering if I should go to San Francisco tomorrow. Margie said she could stay over to help the other friend already scheduled to stay with Elizabeth while I made the vegetable run. The couples went into the bedroom and visited with Elizabeth. The bone-colored sheets with the large butterflies were on the bed. Margie set the table. I called two or three of my vegetable suppliers to remind them of the collection tomorrow. I worried if I should go at all.

After twenty minutes or so, one of the men came out from the bedroom and said that Elizabeth needed me. The others followed him out. She was pleased to say that she needed to go to the toilet. She hoped that meant the diuretic was working. She looked as though she thought it was a long way to the bathroom. I urged her to stay put. Together we managed with the bedpan. She had often helped me with that necessity. I had never helped her.

She was pleased that she passed some urine. I was distressed when I saw how little she gave up and how deep was its color. I feared she had not lost much body fluid yet. She settled back and agreed to take the codeine. Her legs were still hurting her terribly.

The food the friends brought smelled good and I wanted to eat but I was worrying about the trip to San Francisco. Finally, I called Frank. I told him how worried I was. "I can't advise you," he said, strangely, I thought. "But if it were I, I wouldn't go." If that's not advice, I'd like to know what you call it.

The two men guests quickly volunteered to make the vegetable run. They were sure they could manage the old truck. One was a super-annuated Safeway executive, the other a former highway engineer. Both early retirees. I was amused and pleased with the thought of these two bouncing along in that ancient truck with the fresh produce stacked high behind them. I was especially pleased for I was sure they would collect and deliver one of the largest loads of the season. How persistent is our vanity. Original Sin! I hoped they would meet Ella Rigney who became executive director of Raphael House when she was 84 and who lived and worked in that shelter. A better model for them to think about than guaranteed life care!

So it was arranged that they would come back in the morning, do the run, and then give Margie a ride home. Thus she could stay through the night. I checked in on Elizabeth who seemed to be settling down. The couples quickly cleaned up the kitchen. I made some more phone calls. Before I knew it the guests were leaving. Elizabeth had fallen asleep so they didn't speak to her again. Apparently the codeine had been effective in making her more comfortable and bringing some sleep.

As soon as they were gone, I made some more phone calls. I wanted everything to run smoothly about the vegetable run tomorrow. I was anxious about it and troubled. I wasn't really sure they could get along without me! Then I returned to the bedroom again. I stood at the door. Elizabeth lay so still, her head resting deep into the pillows, comfortably, as though the medication had really knocked her out. I went back to the kitchen feeling oddly uneasy. I put away a few things left on the counter. After a moment or two, I said to Margie, "When you get a chance, look in on Elizabeth. See what you think."

She put down what she was doing and went to the bedroom. She came back right away. "I don't think she's breathing," she said.

I rushed into the room. She's all right, I thought. It is just the codeine. She's hardly ever had any strong stuff like that.

"Elizabeth," I whispered. She was very quiet. I sat down on the edge of the bed, our generous comfortable queen size bed. "Liz." I gently took her hand. There was no response. "Oh, Liz. No . . . Margie, call Frank . . . Liz, Liz." I kept calling to her, urging her awake, surely it was only the codeine. My hands raced all over her body, frantically, as though I could, through my frenzied fingers, channel life into her arms, her face, her hair, her breasts, her legs, . . . enough life, enough breath, for another word, another assurance, another touch, another promise. "Oh, Liz. Liz."

Then I heard the unhearable. I thought it happened only in Victorian novels. The death rattle. Breath, her precious, costly, fought-for breath, unmistakably coming from her body, from her lungs, quietly, audibly, through her throat and face. It was as though the last bit of life she possessed, her last breath, she had reserved for me, now that I had found time to be with her. Now our last hour was gone, our last moment. Most of it I had spent on the telephone, arranging, managing, anxious and troubled about many things!

Liz, I was not there with you. I did not hold your hand. The promise I most resolved to keep, I had not kept. "If only," I thought, "if only." And all I had hoped to do and now could never do, never, ever for her, swamped me. Promises made and forgotten. Promises made and never kept. And now this. I was not there. Her hand had no hand to hold. I had left her . . . alone on this side. "Oh, Liz," I whispered against her body, with my words muffled, buried with my face in all of her I could embrace. "Oh, Liz," I breathed, "Liz, forgive me."

Then, with that breath spent, hers and mine, a miracle happened. A miracle for both of us. Here and there from somewhere beyond us both, where promises are never broken and hands are always held. A voice from heaven or in our hearts? A voice speaking to the 'quick and the dead'. A voice, "Take my hand, Elizabeth. Take my hand. Arise, take up your bed and walk."

Her anguished body seemed to unbend from all its burden, straighten out, grow supple again. As she lay there, she seemed once more to be as she was when we first knew each other as a woman and a man in our promises and in our love. In the same moment my hands were quieted, my cries were stilled, my remorse, my guilt was lifted, transmuted into grief, love's servant. Jesus had kept his promise. Forgiveness for the living, promise for the dead. "Take my hand, take my hand—and walk."

In that sweet moment, as I looked across our bed where we had known one another, in sickness and in health, through all these growing years, as I looked across our bed and out through the great window, and beyond our little acre, I saw the light in the fire tower on Mt. St. Helena and I knew that Elizabeth was cradled in the arms of God. And so was I.

"Behold, what manner of love God hath bestowed upon us . . . "

CHAPTER 25

Therefore ... Let Us Love One Another

It was a divine miracle of promises kept which helped me let Elizabeth go. If you also are having trouble in letting her go, but are not much into divine miracles, perhaps it will help you a bit to hear about some human miracles of love which also helped to ease the separation. The line between the two, the human and the divine, the mundane and the miraculous, is very thin. When you hear just a little of what happened around us when the word was out that Elizabeth had responded to the invitation to "get up and walk," I think you will agree with me that there are miracles which love works that are very earthy and near and believable.

By the time Margie reached Frank, who was making a house call on another patient, it was clear to her that Elizabeth had already died. She told him so. Therefore, he did an unusual thing. He did not come racing out to the house. First, he went home. Somehow, on short notice, he and Angie arranged a baby-sitter. Later, aware that someone had come to the front door, I came out from the bedroom. There was not only Frank, but Angie, too. Not only the physician, but the friends. I see them yet, standing there quietly, unobstrusively, waiting for me. The warmth of the embrace which followed still wraps around me like an over-sized wool sweater thrown around my shoulders on a shivering night.

Ros, whom we delighted to call "our pastor," as though we lived in a Scottish village, (he looks grand in his kilts once a year, especially when he is "with beard") made a last call on Elizabeth that night, summoned earnestly from a meeting, but she had already gone. He and Frank and I stood around the bed and made an accidental triangle of caring arms over her, as we reached out for each others' hands and said the Lord's Prayer together. We couldn't seem to manage more spoken words. I thought Elizabeth must feel the support of this human trinity following her with their prayers.

It was only later I learned that Abby, the indoor cat, was beside Elizabeth when she died. She had taken up her post there even before the red rose joined all the artifacts on the sill of the great window. She did not move until the undertaker insisted. When the body was carried from the house, Abby, who was never allowed outdoors, ran along beneath the shrouded stretcher, staying very close and then, once outdoors, broke away and escaped into the night, into the shadowy world of shrubbery and woods. As Margie went after her and comforted her back into the house, I thought to myself how the simple realities and accidents of life break through to distract and ease us through some of life's roughest moments.

* * * * * * * *

"What do we do now?"

I knew what I wanted to do. I knew what would please the children. I knew what would be fitting for Elizabeth. So I went to the telephone. I called John Mitchell. It was getting late.

"John," I said when he finally answered the insistent ringing, "John, Elizabeth is gone."

"O God, no."

"About an hour ago," I said.

"God," he said again. "No. No. I'm glad we didn't turn off the phone tonight." I wondered how anyone could do that any night.

"John," I went on, "do you possibly know a cabinetmaker who could take some time off right away and build a simple casket for her?"

"Make a casket?"

"Yes. Just a simple box. Plain."

John did not reply.

"It doesn't have to be fancy, but . . . "

There was silence between us. I wished I could see his face.

"I can do that," he said hesitantly. And then, quickly, as though he had just figured out how he could, he came on strongly, "Yes. I can do that. I would like to. I will."

Some weeks later he told me that the next morning at breakfast he told Karen, "What have I done? I've promised to build a casket and I don't know the first thing about it. I don't think I've ever seen one up close."

"Well, you better find out . . . and fast," Karen told him.

Later that day he got advice from his friend, Harold Morrison, the undertaker who helped him a lot. John called me about size. How tall was Elizabeth anyway? Practical realities again! He also wanted reassurance about the simplicity, "Even a fancy molding, I couldn't put on her coffin," he said.

Then once again he called. "I just can't use new wood," he said. "I wouldn't dare cause a tree to be cut down, however indirectly, to make a casket for Elizabeth. So I have found some very old wood. Actually, it's first growth redwood tank stock. Beautiful clear wood. Salvaged from a large wine cask. It's perfect."

So John Mitchell, whose friends came to rib him as the "Full Service Contractor—Cradles & Coffins," made a casket for his friend, Elizabeth. It was a beautiful plain box, natural and smooth and gracefully proportioned, with redwood handles and the screws all countersunk and pegged. He was very worried about its weight.

"How many pallbearers will there be?" he asked me urgently the next day or so. "It's going to be heavier than I thought."

"Six," I said.

"Better make it eight, unless they are all young and in good shape."

"That's fine," I said. "I would like to have twenty-eight. There are so many I think of."

The following Sunday afternoon we took Elizabeth back to Berkeley, the scene of the happiest years of her life. Our friend, Dorothy Brooks, who after a career as artist and high school teacher, had been ordained from that congregation, presided with Ros at the service. When she said, "Today, with praise and thanksgiving, we bring Elizabeth home to her little family of the heart," our hearts trembled. Elizabeth's body rested unseen amidst her friends in a redwood casket, hand-rubbed smooth as Ivan's coat, a casket lovingly built and freely given, which had just the faint aroma of burgundy about it. John Mitchell was still fully collaborating with Elizabeth in saving trees.

On the night of Elizabeth's death after I called the children and our sisters and had talked with Mitchell, I called one or two others, including friends from my childhood who live in retirement at Claremont, California. The next morning the phone rang. It was early. The first call. I answered it.

"This is Davie," a lively voice announced.

"Davie?" I questioned.

"Yes. Davie. Remember me? We are so sorry."

It was the professor colleague of over thirty years ago, the former Holmes Professor of Old Testament Criticism and Interpretation at Yale, who now laughingly disclaims any responsibility for the decoration of our bridal suite at the pastors' school. He and I had had disagreements over the years, the relationship had cooled, communication had broken down.

"Davie," I said, "thank you. Thank you from my heart." He also lives in Claremont. The sad news not only spread quickly but it brought healing, too. Forgiveness unspoken, promises refreshed.

When most of the family had arrived we visited the little cemetery a mile and a half up the road from our place. It was given for the use of residents of this valley on the condition that the price of the lots never be increased. Barbara Wurz, who before her unseasonable death, kindly and efficiently tended to many matters in this valley, including the cemetery, met us there with a plot plan spread out on the dusty hood of her hard used Continental and a very long measuring tape.

She explained that a plot for four graves costs $12.50, but that one for ten graves is $25. So we splurged. There is a wide selection of sites for, on average, there is only one grave dug a year. She told us that the fence was the most reliable guide and to measure from it to mark out a chosen plot. We looked around and finally stepped out a space which was protected by a large tree with a few smaller ones of promising appearance. It also appeared reasonably free of poison oak! It was also within sight of the highway for Elizabeth could not resist running to the windows when we lived on busy Ashby Avenue if she heard a siren. The traffic fascinated her, too, as it backed up at rush hour.

After we had chosen the spot, Layton, standing near the sight, said, indicating a particular spot, "This will have to be the head of the grave."

"Why?" his sister asked.

"Come and see," he answered.

We all moved en masse to where he stood.

"Look through the trees," he said.
We did. There, clearly visible, was Mt. St. Helena.

* * * * * * * *

There were many amusing human things which happened then and in the ensuing days to give lighter colors to our grief. The night of Elizabeth's death I asked Frank and Angie to clear out Elizabeth's medicine. We had just purchased three month's supply of vitamins. They swept all that up, too, as they cleaned out our medicine cabinet. I am sure it was put to good use. Or maybe Frank doesn't believe in vitamins. I must remember to ask him someday.

A few weeks after the burial a friend in St. Helena, who keeps a prize garden, took her helper and visited the cemetery with appropriate tools. Together they planted California poppy seeds around the grave. Then later, unknown to me, five friends of Elizabeth, including one who is a professional gardener, friends who for years celebrated with Elizabeth their common February birthday month, also visited the cemetery, and planted California poppies around the grave. Then in the Spring when daughter Leigh came from St. Louis where she once worked in a nursery, she also brought wild flower seeds, including California poppies, which she carefully planted. When I am asked and even when I am not, I am pleased to assure all of these people that the poppies have done very well, indeed, very prolific. Until now, however, I have never confessed to any of them that I do not really know that it is their seeds and their planting which has been so successful!

The revolution of the sixties for which Berkeley is honored or detested was contagious. Elizabeth joined her friend, Mary Eakin, my associate of many years who preceded her in death, in rebelling against the assumption that women's life in the church must always be task oriented. They established "the Friday Group" which outlawed any tasks or dues or money raising. It was to be for busy women, already full to their ears with work in the church and community and vocation, who needed time to be nurtured and listened to and supported in a friendly environment.The Friday Group has thrived for 25 years. When they learned of the serious nature of Elizabeth's illness, they used some of the hours of a weekend retreat to create a banner for her. On a sky blue and earth-toned background they placed all the birds she saw from her window and much else. They sent a small delegation to visit Elizabeth and present it. Our sons were both home at the time and made a great celebration of hanging it.

That handsome banner hung beside the casket at the church service. Nancy McKay carried it out, leading the pallbearers, as the church emptied to triumphant trumpet music. The next day when it was almost time for everyone to gather at the cemetery, Nancy and Dorothy Brooks noticed that the banner was nowhere in sight. They found it, sped to the cemetery, pulled their car as near to the great tree as they could, took off their shoes (I hope), climbed up on the hood (it was a new car!) and hung the banner on a snaggle-toothed branch they could just barely reach. It was lovely in the breeze and they were content.

There were several events I would have vetoed if I had had the chance. I am forever grateful I did not have the chance. Ros Gordon invited others to speak beside the grave and then sang the 23rd Psalm to the simple tune from the Scottish Psalter. Joan and Bob, my nephew, alerted by their son, contrary to my expressed wishes, abandoned a European sailing vacation and came home. Another nephew, the one who gave me the truck and who owns the most elegant car in the family, drove in from Colorado and insisted on chauffeuring me everywhere. Son Christopher, in Germany and isolated from these days by distance, arranged for a friend, a gifted San Francisco pianist, to play Brahms' *Intermezzo* in the church before the prayers. Daughter Leigh fashioned a bouquet for the casket from the flowers and greenery each one of us selected from our garden. Son Layton wrote a poem. Sue and her younger daughter, Sophia, made a one day round trip from New York City to be with us. Sophia, age eleven, held my hand.

While we were in Berkeley for the service, Amador and his brothers moved in and manicured our "backyard," so it became a garden. And there, the next day after the burial, our Alexander Valley friends, the Hafners, who had raced to the house the night Elizabeth died, served a choice luncheon for everyone.

Ready to go to the cemetery, I remembered the red rose I had placed in the window for Elizabeth six days earlier. I could not believe my eyes when I found it still fresh. I took it to the cemetery with me. As I placed it on the casket and turned back from the grave to join my children, only two faces caught my eye. I thought how amazed and pleased Elizabeth would be. John Mitchell and Frank Mueller. But neither one had any business being there for it was eleven o'clock on a busy Monday morning.

It was not only close friends who deeply loved Elizabeth who were miracle workers with their caring. Others, less closely connected, did more than they will ever guess. Sometime, unknown to me, our neighbor, Dave Korte, who is a skilled back hoe operator, went to the cemetery and prepared the grave. No artificial turf, no fancy awning. He simply dug a neat deep grave and thoughtfully moved the soil a distance away behind a clump of bushes. Then, again without my knowledge, after the service, another neighbor, Jim Bushnell, filled the grave. My nephew, the one with the truck and the elegant automobile, has spent his life with heavy machinery. He stayed with others at the grave. He told me he had never seen anyone handle heavy machinery with such skill and move soil with such gentleness. The grave was closed.

A List Composed on Sacred Ground

Even the traffic rumbling by
has a muted quality
in this simple valley plot.
Nothing is out of place.
There are bluejays, quail and sparrows,

moles and burrowing shrews
insects that eat wood, and flesh
eating ones that're forgotten
long before the most isolate
human corpse is lost in

the memory of the person who
last perceived it. Cows graze
up to the fence and still
low in the evenings
as they used to. Their dull eyes

shine in the brilliance
of California's escaping
full sunset. And the coyotes
will not dig as deep as
you are. I can't imagine rain

or ruts in the drive, but
it will come. As mustard flowers
will brighten the vineyards
that encircle this wooded place
like a promise.

Maurice Layton Barr

Epilogue

After the Ending and Before the Beginning

When I returned from the cemetery, as I told you at the outset, Frank met me in the short hallway which connects the kitchen and our bedroom, the room with the great window looking out at Mt. St. Helena. He suggested it was time for us to talk. He asked what I thought had happened to us.

I have had a lot of time to think about his question.

I have answered it in terms of what happened to Elizabeth and me, refreshed within and forever by the forgiveness and the promises, human and divine, in the aging of love. I have also answered it in terms of what happened to me, and my being discovered and loved afresh in that ultimate intimacy Elizabeth had long known.

But Frank's question was what had happened to *us*, to me and him, and Mitchell, too, I suppose, and all those other friends, members of "the little family of the heart," some of whom were gathering at that moment on the patio outside, eating potato salad and drinking good wine and smelling the roses and talking about all these things that had happened, about Elizabeth and her long dying.

Hannah Arendt speaks of forgiveness and promise but she doesn't stop there. It takes two to tangle. She suggests how other people are inevitably connected:

185

*Both faculties, forgiving and promising, depend on the pres-
ence and acting of others for no one can forgive himself and no
one can be bound by a promise made only to himself.*

So this informal community of loving relationships, like marriage, is also an adventure in forgiveness, friends held together
by the stout webbing of that love which, in its maturity, takes
the initiative and enters into the pain of others.

In our first encounter six years earlier in that bedroom where
Elizabeth had died, "Dr. Mueller" and I had not stood there in
warm human embrace, acknowledging our common humanity. I
wasn't even standing up! It was he who stood there, looming
over me with all the authority of his profession. I was angry to
be powerless before this smart young stranger. He came with the
power of his authority.

Six years later he had come voluntarily to help lay Elizabeth
to rest. I was amazed. Doctors in our society do not often so
publicly celebrate their powerlessness. All his power as authority over Elizabeth had now been dissipated, lost, given away.

Yet he still stood there with power. The power of his love. It
was love, entering into another's pain, that had moved him to
arrange transportation for her that day when I was away and he
thought he should see her. It was love, entering into another's
pain that had made him postpone less urgent appointments when
she was needing someone besides me to talk with unhurriedly.
It was love that brought him today to "this simple valley plot."

John Mitchell, also, was in the cemetery that morning. That
surprised me, too. Like Mueller, his business was done. The
casket would soon be lowered and forever out of sight. Like
Mueller we had first called him to our house to exercise the
power of his authority, his expertise. We did not know him either. We wanted the old bathroom remodelled, but we couldn't
do it ourselves. We needed help. He came with the authority of
his skill and experience.

But it was love which built the porch around the tree; it was
love which dreamed up and installed garden faucets Elizabeth
could manage; it was love which arranged tolerable shade against
the summer sun; it was love which, at the end, hunted all over
the valley for recyclable wood for Elizabeth's casket so no axe
would touch a living tree in her name. It was love that brought
him also that September morning to the wooded place with the
"bluejays, quail and sparrows." These two young men met us in
our plight and they loved us, taking the initiative and entering
into our pain.

So there we had been in the cemetery together, a vignette on the last page, Mueller and Mitchell and Elizabeth in her casket and me. Then in my mind that design did not fade out at the edges but broadened into a wider and richer focus. I saw all these other people, a great company of friends.

Endless trips they had made to us and gifts they had brought and time they had spent and tears they had shed, taking the initiative and entering into our pain until it was their pain, too. We had been loved with forgiveness and promise. That love which is "patient and kind, not jealous or boastful, not arrogant or rude, not irritable or resentful," may well find its first stirring in erotic love and its delight in philia love, but it displays its transforming power in "agape" love, "which bears all things, believes all things, hopes all things, endures all things."

Perhaps the physician and the contractor were the primary symbols, agents of my enlightenment, because neither of them by birth or custom was committed to loving us. Neither one was a blood relative. Neither one had we met in church. Neither one was of our generation. Neither one was a neighbor. But there was something else: these two made very clear that you do not have to reverse your collar or join up with a religious order to be instruments of redemptive love. "Doctor, lawyer, merchant, chief . . ." Grace-filled love flowing from them. Some days more, some days less. And they didn't even know it. They probably don't even believe it now. The priesthood of all believers!

I have only tried to tell the story of what happened to Elizabeth and me, love's grand aging: *eros, philia, agape!* One's own story is really the only story one knows for sure. What about the others? What about Frank? He started all this ruminating by suggesting it was time we talked about what happened to us? I've told about what happened to me. But what happened to him? I do not know. I have only one clue to venture, one incident to recall again.

Ten days or so before Elizabeth's family and friends stood together in the cemetery and gave thanks to God for Elizabeth, she and I were in Frank's office, as I have already told you. He looked at her as though he wished he could hide the despair in his eyes and the helplessness in his hands. She was very sick. He knew it. She knew it. I did not.

You will recall that hard poignant moment when Frank finally spoke. "Elizabeth, will you do me a favor?"

"If I can, of course," she replied.

"Do you think you could make it over to Santa Rosa and see Dr. Price?"

"Oh, Frank," she gasped.

"I know it is quite a trip. Especially on a hot day. But I wish you would."

"Oh, Frank," she protested.

"I'm afraid maybe I've lost my objectivity. I need to have you see Dr. Price. For my sake."

There was a long silence. I was thinking that the loss of his objectivity, scandal perhaps in the medical fraternity, was the medicine that was helping her now. I am sure Elizabeth was thinking, how could she, always so pressed for words about what mattered to her most, tell him that he had all the medicine she needed. How could she let him know without any mistake how sorry she was that this was so hard on him. How could she say "thank you" for his love and care all through these six years, say it so he could clearly hear her and not ever forget she loved him, too.

She broke the silence quietly, "Will you make the appointment or shall I?"

She went.

It was a blistering hot day.

Four days later she was dead.

It is little wonder that Frank stopped me in the hallway between the kitchen and the bedroom with the great window looking out at Mt. St. Helena, stopped me there after we had buried Elizabeth, and suggested it was time we had a talk, a talk about what had happened to us.

Love in its aging enlarges its sweep.

And when love's arms are stilled, love in its aging sends grief to embrace us.

And when we are stilled in the stillness of death, love in its aging increases in power, going from strength to strength, until it pushes the stone away.

* * * * * * * *

Ivan, the outdoor cat, still comes occasionally to the dressing room door. I let her in. She sniffs around, then looks up at me. I tell her, "She's not here, Ivan. She's gone." She waits around a moment or two and then goes her way. It's not easy to get used to the vacancy.